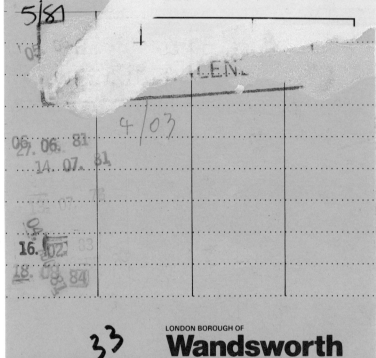

ESCAPE!

ALSO BY RICHARD DEACON

The Private Life of Mr Gladstone
Madoc and the Discovery of America
John Dee
William Caxton: The First English Editor
Matthew Hopkins: Witchfinder-General
A History of the British Secret Service
A History of the Russian Secret Service
A History of the Chinese Secret Service
The Israeli Secret Service
The Silent War:
A History of Western Naval Intelligence
The British Connection:
Russia's Manipulation of British Individuals and Institutions
Spy!

RICHARD DEACON

ESCAPE!

This book is based upon the BBC Television series
ESCAPE
produced by FRANK COX

Scripts written by

SHANE CONNAUGHTON
'Banned' – Donald Woods

HUGH CONNOR
'The Cartland Murder'
'The Poisoned Gift' – Kim Philby

JOHN ELLIOT
'Hijack to Mogadishu'

ARTHUR JONES
'Into Thin Air' – Lord Lucan

MARTIN WORTH
'The Lion's Mouth' – Alfred Hinds

Research by
BERNARD ADAMCZEWSKI
BILLIE MORTON

BRITISH BROADCASTING CORPORATION

904 DEAC
100397 975

Published by the
British Broadcasting Corporation
35 Marylebone High Street
London W1M 4AA

ISBN 0 563 17772 1

First published 1980

© Richard Deacon 1980

Printed and bound in Great Britain by
W & J Mackay Limited, Chatham

Contents

I
'The Poisoned Gift'
Kim Philby

'After the third man, the fourth man, after the fourth man the fifth man, who is the fifth man, always beside you?'

CYRIL CONNOLLY

Rumours of a super-mole high up inside the British Establishment had persisted in both London and Washington ever since the two Foreign Office men, Donald Maclean and Guy Burgess, defected to Moscow in 1951.

The Establishment has been badly shaken by that incident, but its principals had tried to preserve the traditional stiff upper lip by pretending that it was quite impossible that there was another traitor, still undetected, in their ranks. Any suggestions of a mole still at large were treated with disdainful denials.

This attitude angered Washington where both in the State Department and in the recently created Central Intelligence Agency (CIA) there were officers who had convinced themselves that there was a highly-placed secret Soviet agent either inside the British Foreign Office or the Secret Service. In fact, suspicions of this sort had begun to crystallise a few years before Maclean and Burgess suddenly left Britain. The interrogation of the defecting Russian cipher clerk, Igor Gouzenko, shortly after the end of World War II had pointed in the direction of an unnamed Soviet agent working in a senior position in MI 5, the British counter-espionage organisation.

Some thought the Russian had confused MI 5 with MI 6 (the British Secret Service operating overseas). Others pooh-poohed much of his evidence. Some Americans, both in the CIA and Hoover's FBI, suspected the mole was in the diplomatic service rather than MI 6. The truth was that the man who skilfully drew attention away from MI 5 and MI 6 and suggested a closer look should be taken at certain senior British diplomats was MI 6's liaison officer with both the CIA and the FBI. This man, appointed to Washington in the summer of 1949, was none other than Harold Adrian Russell Philby, more generally known as 'Kim' Philby.

In 1949 this thirty-seven-year-old Intelligence officer seemed at the threshold of a distinguished career. In some quarters he was discreetly whispered about as a possible future chief of the Secret Service. Certainly he had risen quickly enough for such a prize to have been within his grasp within the next ten years. A knighthood would inevitably have followed and, in retirement, possibly even a Fellowship at some Cambridge college.

Philby had been born in India on New Year's Day, 1912. His father, Harry St John Philby, was then a member of the British-controlled Indian Civil Service. The nickname of 'Kim' was chosen from the character created by Rudyard Kipling. It was ironic that Kipling's 'Kim' should also have been mixed up in espionage. Philby's father was very different from the usual type of highly dedicated, conservative and discreet Indian Civil Service men of the days of the Raj. There were in the father signs of rebellion and deviousness which were later to show themselves in his son, though the latter was much cleverer in disguising them. For St John Philby suddenly developed a passion for the Arab world, left India and spent his remaining years often living like a Moslem and roaming the deserts of Arabia. He was frequently critical of British policy towards the Moslem world and, at a time when the shadows of approaching war were cast over Britain, was regarded in some quarters as being not only pro-Arab, but pro-Nazi as well.

Kim was brought up chiefly by his mother in London, where he attended his father's old school, Westminster. From there he went to Trinity College, Cambridge, which, in the 1930s, was seething with radical revolt against the Establishment generally and in which both the town and university communist parties were vigorously supported by a number of dons as well as many undergraduates. Philby was among them and it was in this period that he started to learn one of the Slav languages. As to the exact moment when he decided to make a secret commitment to the cause of Soviet communism, this must be a matter of conjecture. Some assert he was recruited by a don at Cambridge, others that he was brought into the Russian espionage network whilst on a visit to Vienna. It is perhaps only fair to give his own version:

The first thirty years of my work for the cause in which I believed [the USSR] were, from the beginning, spent underground. This long phase started in Central Europe in June, 1933; it ended in Lebanon in January, 1963. Only then was I able to emerge in my true colours, the colours of a Soviet Intelligence officer.

The truly astonishing thing was how Philby managed to bamboozle people into believing that he had never had any contacts with communism and that his thinking was passionately anti-communist. There are at least four senior ex-members of MI 6 still living who knew he had been a communist at Cambridge and that he had married a communist – Litzi Friedman. Lord Dacre (Hugh Trevor-Roper, a wartime member of the British Secret Service) has stated that, when he learned Philby had been appointed to MI 6, he was astonished . . . for my old Oxford friend had told me years before that his travelling companion [Philby] was a communist . . . I was surprised because no one was more fanatically anti-communist at that time than the regular members of the two security services, MI 5 and MI 6.

It was even more surprising when one considers that Britain was in 1939 at war with Germany whose ally was then the Soviet Union. Only later did Germany break that pact by invading Russia in the early summer of 1941.

Astonishing it certainly was. Yet there were a few others in MI 6 who knew about Philby's antecedents just as Lord Dacre did. Someone who had been with him at Cambridge said: 'I knew how he had felt about things as an undergraduate, but I supposed that was just a bit of youthful lunacy which he had grown out of. After all, others had been pretty Bolshie while at the university.'

It was quite true that there had been widespread Marxist influences at Cambridge (and Oxford, too) in the early thirties, some of the dons being even more adulatory about the Soviet system than those they taught. But, despite this, only a small minority became active communists. It was Philby himself who was to show later how such a small minority can wield great power and influence.

He had come down from Cambridge in 1933 and made a trip to Vienna. There he not only made friends with a number of communists, but became passionately interested in Austrian politics. Perhaps some of the incidents he witnessed in Vienna caused him to swing even more positively leftwards in his opinions. He saw the bloody clashes between the rival private armies of the *Heimwehr* of Prince Stahremberg and the Schutzbund of the Socialists. It was here that he met Litzi Friedman, a young Austrian Jewish girl who had just secured a divorce from a fanatical communist. She was herself a committed communist and in some danger of arrest by the authorities who were rigorously rounding up left-wingers.

In what must appear as a chivalrous gesture, Philby decided to marry Litzi, thereby providing her with a British passport so that she could leave Austria. The pair were married on 24 February 1934, in the Vienna Town Hall. Together they returned to England.

Yet this very act, which was in no way kept secret from his many British friends, casts some doubt on the authenticity of Philby's statement that he became a Soviet agent in 1933. If this is true, it seems remarkably strange that his Soviet controller would allow him to marry. Philby himself has since stated in his book, *My Silent War*, that he was 'given the job of penetrating British Intelligence, and told it did not matter how long I took to do the job'. He has given no other details of his recruitment. But marrying a foreign communist solely to give her a British passport seems an odd way of starting such an assignment.

However, once he had returned to Britain, Philby set about repudiating any communist opinions he may have held and avoiding those earlier contacts who had communist associations. He took the utmost care to give an impression of having veered sharply to the right politically. He mixed in orthodox Conservative circles and by 1936 he had become a member of the Anglo-German Fellowship, a society which had close and friendly relations with Germany's Nazi regime. It included in its membership several distinguished peers, notably Lord Nuffield and the Marquesses of Londerry and Lothian.

One method of obtaining an entrée into Intelligence circles was through journalism, especially as a foreign correspondent. This was, of course, simply a possible short cut into the Secret Service and no guarantee of entry. Most newspapers disliked having anyone on their staffs who was mixed up in Intelligence work, though often in the foreign field they had to put up with them. For instance, *The Times* in the twenties and thirties had many of its correspondents overseas actively working for some branch or other of British Intelligence.

So Philby took a sub-editorial job with a respectable monthly magazine, *The Review of Reviews*, with the aim of paving the way for a job on *The Times*. In 1934 and 1935 he made two trips to Spain, taking his wife with him on each occasion. When the Spanish civil war broke out in 1936, Philby made plans to cover it. He worked feverishly to obtain commissions as a freelance journalist from various sources, including, of course, *The Times*. In February 1937, he arrived in Spain as a correspondent covering the forces of General Franco and he quickly became a firm favourite with the Nationalist officers. Within a few months Philby had proved his journalistic talents sufficiently to get *The Times* to make him their fully accredited correspondent.

At last he was in a position to start proving to the Russians that he could justify the trust they had apparently reposed in him. Being attached to their 'enemy forces' in Spain (the USSR had already intervened on the Republican side), he would be able from time to time to provide them with intelligence. As to how this was passed on to the Russians remains his own secret to this day. It must have given him cause for quiet satisfaction that some of his colleagues suspected him of being an undercover British agent, because, said one of them, 'he was always so eager to get rather more details on troop movements and numbers engaged than any other among us'.

Quite often he would slip across the border into France, ostensibly for brief relaxation, but nobody seems to recall exactly what he did or where he went on these occasions. He may well have met his Soviet courier in St Jean de Luz.

When the civil war ended he returned to London. The cynicism of Soviet policy in this period is clearly indicated by the Russians' sudden lack of interest in Spain as, with the Republicans clearly losing the war, they abandoned their left-wing allies in that country. Republican Spain was sacrificed to pave the way for the signing of the Soviet-German Pact in the late summer of 1939. Once this was achieved, any hope of a Franco-British-Soviet alliance was destroyed and World War II became inevitable.

Philby went overseas again in October 1939, this time as a war correspondent for *The Times* to the British Expeditionary Force in Arras. Sir Fitzroy Maclean, recalling meeting him at this time, says that he wore Franco's Red Cross of Military Valour with his uniform and that he was 'a dark, good-looking, rather saturnine young man of twenty-eight, much in demand with London luncheon hostesses longing for a first-hand account of what it had been like at the front'.

It was about this time that he was first approached to join British Intelligence. He has been somewhat reluctant to say how this happened, but his own version is that he had 'watched various irons I had put in the fire, nudging one or other of them as they appeared to hot up'. Then came a call by telephone to the Foreign Editor of *The Times*, asking whether he was 'available for war work'. Soon afterwards Philby found himself

in the forecourt of the St Ermin's Hotel, near St James's Park station, talking to Miss Marjorie Maxse . . . an interesting elderly lady . . . She spoke with authority, and was evidently in a position at least to recommend me for 'interesting' employment . . . I passed the first examination . . . At our second meeting she turned up accompanied by Guy Burgess, whom I knew well. I was put through my paces again . . . Before we parted Miss Maxse informed me that, if I agreed, I should sever my connection with *The Times* and report for duty to Guy Burgess at an address in Caxton Street, in the same block as the St Ermin's Hotel.

Miss Maxse (later Dame Marjorie Maxse) was chief organisation officer of the Conservative Party Central Office from 1921–39. From 1940–4 she was vice-chairman of the Women's Voluntary Service. Guy Burgess, a Cambridge friend of Philby's, had already been recruited into the Soviet network and had infiltrated to a marginal extent the precincts of MI 5 and MI 6, sending in reports to the former and maintaining close contacts with personnel in the latter.

The manner of Philby's recruitment via Miss Maxse may sound like a piece of Soviet propaganda. But even if it was true that he was interviewed by her, the initiative for his recruitment came from quite a different quarter. The first overture to Philby was made by a Captain Leslie Sheridan in the War Office. Recruitment in the British Intelligence ranks still came mainly from the ex-officer ranks and, though investigations into the background of recruits were still carried out, they were all rather perfunctory, with family names counting for rather more than they should.

It was all rather odd [wrote one MI 6 member, John Whitwell], but everything struck me as odd in those early days – including my manner of entry into the Secret Service. I was an Army officer who had had some experience in the Intelligence side of the General Staff. One day in 1929 I phoned an officer in Military Intelligence to try to fix up a job as an interpreter for a man who had left the Army. The sequel was that I met an Intelligence officer who, after several further talks, suggested that I should resign my commission and enter this field . . . But nobody at this stage gave me tips on how to work as a spy or how to make contact with likely sources, or how to worm information out of them.

Later this very same MI 6 agent was alarmed when he learned from a contact man in Vienna how his predecessors in British Intelligence had behaved. One of them was in the habit of worrying his superiors by periodically going off on drinking bouts for days on end. On one occasion this alcoholic, who should never have been selected as a spy, was picked up by the Austrian police for being offensive and clapped into a cell. In his briefcase, which luckily had not been searched, were all kinds of confidential documents which he had collected earlier in the day.

Yet, despite ample evidence of the somewhat casual and unprofessional approach to recruitment in the Secret Service, it is still incredible that Philby should have been allowed to join. MI 5, Britain's counter-espionage service, had a file on him, but whether this was produced, minimised or suppressed is not clear. All that is known is that Captain Guy Liddell, a senior executive in MI 5, gave him clearance.

Philby himself must have been worried about MI 5 reports concerning him about the time of his appointment, for, as he has since admitted, his trips to Spain had been suggested to him and financed by the USSR in the first place. In 1940 Walter Krivitsky, head of Soviet Military Intelligence for Western Europe, and formerly resident director of their intelligence network based in Holland, defected to the United States. He made a number of revelations to a US Senate Committee, but some of these more directly concerned Britain. Eventually he was interviewed by MI 5 and he revealed that the Russians had sponsored a young British journalist in Spain during the civil war.

It should not have been difficult for MI 5 to have identified this man as Philby by a process of careful elimination of war correspondents in Spain. The extraordinary thing is that MI 5 had been the most efficient and ruthless organisation for stamping out subversive communism in the previous decade, yet either they 'missed' Philby, or someone inside MI 5 protected him. Lord Dacre took the view that 'although I myself knew of Philby's communist past, it would never have occurred to me, at that time, to hold it against him . . . My own view, like that of my contemporaries, was that our superiors were lunatic in their anti-communism.'

This is a debatable contention. It might have been a logical, if not a legitimate, argument in, say, the following year after Germany had invaded Russia. But at this time Germany and the USSR had a pact. In any event, to Philby's communist past had to be added the record of his pro-German activities (he actually edited the Anglo-German Fellowship's journal) and his pro-Franco sympathies. Then there was the fact that his father had not only been known to express fascist views, but had for a brief time early in World War II been an inmate of Brixton Prison under Regulation 18 B, which covered people suspected of being sympathetic towards the enemy, Germany.

Philby was first recruited into Section D of the British Secret Service. This organisation – the 'D' was for Destruction – had been set up in 1938 under Colonel Lawrence Grand. It was intended, as its name implied, to be an aggressive unit aimed at inflicting damage on the enemy by sabotage. But, though the ideas behind this may have been sound and imaginative, the planning and execution were mediocre and by the middle of 1940 the section was doomed. With its collapse Philby was moved to a new organisation which had been created after the German armies swept across Europe. This was the SOE (Special Operations Executive), designed to establish contacts with Resistance and other anti-Nazi activists in occupied Europe. Philby actually became an instructor at the SOE secret school at Beaulieu in Hampshire where prospective agents were given training for clandestine activities in France, Belgium, Holland and other Nazi-occupied territories. But this was not at all to his liking and he knew that, if he was to further the cause of his Soviet masters, he must get back into the mainstream of the Secret Service.

He managed to manipulate this by getting himself asked to lunch with his father and Colonel Vivian, the deputy head of MI 6. The outcome was a job in MI 6 and from then onwards he plotted his own promotion by shrewdly and calculatingly playing off one colleague against another. He also had friends in MI 5 so that he was able to stir up mischief between these two departments of the Security Services. It was all achieved with the minimum of fuss and no ostentatious intrigue – a nod here and a wink there. The portrait gradually emerged to his superiors of a man, wise beyond his years, who was able to see through the follies of his elders and check the over-enthusiasm of his juniors.

The wartime Secret Service grew to such an extent that its headquarters at Broadway in London were too small for its home-based staff. Annexes were set up all over the place, one being the offices at St Albans where Section V was established. This was the section of the Service which dealt with operations in the Iberian Peninsula. It was here that Philby was drafted on the strength of his knowledge and experience of Spanish affairs.

There can be no doubt whatsoever that Philby was a competent operator, clear-minded and efficient as far as his work for MI 6 was concerned. He ingratiated himself with the head of the service, Major-General (then Colonel) Sir Stewart Menzies and was, of course, popular with the wartime university recruits. He had great personal charm and it was this valuable asset which probably disarmed so many of his critics and to a large extent caused his friends later on to insist that Philby could not possibly be a Soviet agent.

Kim Philby with his head in bandages. The photograph was taken during the Spanish Civil War in December 1937, after he had narrowly escaped death when his car was bombed. The three other occupants were all killed

Kim Philby

Anthony Blunt

Guy Burgess

Donald Maclean

Such distinguished and authoritative assessors of ability as Lord Dacre and Sir Fitzroy Maclean have paid tribute to Philby's talents in MI 6. The former said, 'I never doubted that, within the Service, Philby was the man of the future . . . I was convinced that he was being groomed to head the Service'. Sir Fitzroy has referred to Philby's 'remarkably successful career in the Secret Intelligence Service'.

By this time Philby had left his Austrian wife and was living with a girl named Aileen Furse: this no doubt was one way of trying to obliterate his communist past. Towards the end of the war Philby was made the head of an entirely new section of the Service, Section IX, which was intended to concentrate on keeping a watch on the intrigues and espionage of Soviet Russia and to some extent engage in spying operations against the Soviet bloc. Already it was felt that the USSR would soon take the place of Germany as the major threat to British interests.

So during the latter part of the war Philby was able to check or destroy any moves by MI 6 which compromised the Soviet Union. To this day it is still not clear to what extent his activities were against the national interest, or who gained most from them – the British or the Russians. But after the war it was a different story. It is now abundantly clear that Philby did his utmost to sabotage all anti-Soviet activities coming within the orbit of Section IX and that he also managed to subvert some projects of the British Naval Intelligence Division. Then in the summer of 1945, Philby faced his first major crisis since Walter Krivitsky had intimated that the Russians were using a British journalist as one of their agents in Spain. A minor Russian diplomat, Konstantin Volkov, had made a secret approach to the British Vice-Consul in Istanbul asking for asylum. At the same time he intimated that he was an undercover officer of the NKVD (the predecessor of the KGB) and that he could supply details of two Soviet agents who were working in the Foreign Office in London and a third who was a senior member of MI 5.

This must have sent an icy shiver down Philby's spine when the head of the Secret Service asked for suggestions as to how this delicate business should be handled. Although he did not answer to the vague description of any of this trio of spies, it was always possible that Volkov might have made an error and confused MI 6 with MI 5. In any event the revelations of the identities of any of these people could be a major blow for the Russians and in the long term very easily seal Philby's own doom.

An important point about Volkov's request for asylum was that he stipulated that any communications concerning him should be sent to London via the diplomatic bag and not on any account by telegraph as the Russians had broken most of the British ciphers. This should have alerted the authorities to a very serious breach of their own security, yet nothing seems to have been done about it. Fortunately for Philby, his own suggestion that he should himself go to Istanbul to investigate Volkov was blandly accepted by Sir Stewart Menzies, though only after the man Menzies wished to send had declined on the somewhat surprising grounds that he disliked flying!

Truly Philby had many lucky escapes. One must assume that he lost no time in tipping off the Russians about the traitor in their midst. For from that moment Volkov disappeared completely and his name was removed from the Soviet Consulate lists. By the time Philby arrived in Istanbul and asked to be put in touch with Volkov, the Russian Consulate told a perplexed British Consulate official that 'Volkov is in Moscow'. Shortly afterwards there was a report of a heavily-bandaged man being taken aboard a Russian aircraft at Istanbul.

Philby was able to return to London and get away with the suggestion that most probably the Russians had suspected Volkov for some time, had kept watch on him and had his rooms bugged. By now Philby had obtained his divorce from Litzi, who had gone to East Germany, and he then married Aileen Furse. In the following New Year's honours list he was awarded the OBE.

It was during his next two postings that Philby was able to wreak most damage to the Western cause, for, with the war against Germany ended, the USSR was no longer an ally and the Cold War had started. From this point onwards Philby could not claim that, in helping the Russians, he was also helping to defeat the common enemy, Germany. Ironically, his immediate posting was to Istanbul as controlling officer of the MI 6 station in that area. This was soon succeeded in the summer of 1949 with an appointment to the United States where he was instructed to act as liaison officer between the British Secret Service and the CIA. At that time there were certain joint CIA–MI 6 projects in Europe. One was concerned with developing links with underground Ukrainian nationalist movements (there had long been sporadic resistance to Soviet administration in Russia's Ukraine province); another aimed at lending support to the clandestine Albanian Resistance organisation which sprang up after Albania acquired a communist government. Philby was privy to both projects. However, he was also concerned with counter-espionage, which brought him into contact with Edgar Hoover's FBI, and the need to find out about Soviet espionage inside the USA, a subject of paramount importance in American eyes since the trials of the nuclear spies.

Menzies was shortly to retire from MI 6 and few regarded his successor, the ill-fated Major-General Sinclair, as anything other than a temporary head of the Service. Philby was within sight of the supreme prize – the post of 'C', as the head of MI 6 was known. All he had to do was to ingratiate himself with the Americans and ensure smooth relations between MI 6, the CIA and the FBI. A difficult task, it was true, for already some Americans (especially Edgar Hoover) were beginning to suspect the presence of traitors in the British Establishment.

It must have been at this time that Philby came under great mental strain. Graham Greene, the novelist, who also served in MI 6 during World War II, later compared Kim to those Catholics who, in the reign of Elizabeth I, 'worked for the victory of Spain'. Like them, he added, 'Philby has a chilling certainty in the correctness of his judgement, the logical fanaticism of a man who, having once found a faith, is not going to lose it because of the injustices or cruelties inflicted by erring human instruments'. This is very far from being an accurate analogy. The fanatical, dedicated communist does not as a rule make a good agent: his very fanaticism, his inability to dissemble sooner or later give him away. The Russians, when employing foreigners as agents, are interested only in results, not in the personal convictions of their undercover employees. After all, once they have positively compromised their agent, they can always use the discipline of blackmail tactics to keep him in his place. In any event Philby was no idealist, not one who would willingly forgo Western comforts and delights for communist beliefs.

His charm had begun to wear a little thin by the late forties; it seemed as though he needed to fortify himself with a great deal of liquor to maintain his sprightly talk. Doubtless the Volkov incident had shattered his nerves and, with Russia being regarded as a potential enemy by both the USA and Britain, his path as a double-agent was increasingly hazardous.

While he needed to impress London by his ability to get along with his opposite number in America, he was also required to sabotage the joint CIA–MI 6 operations and to put up a smokescreen which would prevent the FBI from ascertaining the identities of those Britons who were purloining their secrets. If his intervention in the Ukraine was minimal, it is certain that he was able to direct the Russians to track down and kill Stefan Bandera. In his own account of this affair, he blames the CIA for the assassination of Bandera. It was long afterwards that Bogdan Stashinsky defected to the Americans and admitted he had killed Bandera with a nerve-gas gun on the instructions of the KGB. But in sabotaging the Albanian operation Philby was responsible for betraying not one, but a score or more of agents smuggled into that country. One after another they were shot down as they arrived by parachute.

At the same time he was ingeniously thinking up names of phoney suspects inside the British Diplomatic Service to make both the Americans and the British look for the now suspected top traitor in the wrong places. His task was not made any easier by the fact that MI 5 also had a man in Washington.

To add to these problems Philby was landed with an even greater one which his own wife prophesied would end in disaster. This was the arrival in Washington of Guy Burgess, his old college friend from his Cambridge days. This occurred in the summer of 1950 when Philby had moved with his growing family into a large house in Nebraska Avenue. Burgess asked

Philby if he would put him up at his home until he found himself other accommodation. It was then that Philby committed what, with hindsight, must have seemed an elementary and yet monumental error: he not only agreed to Burgess's suggestion, but even proposed that Burgess could stay on indefinitely. Philby, of course, knew that Burgess had a reputation for drunkenness, homosexual promiscuity and indiscretion. Not long before this Burgess had made a trip to Gibraltar and Tangier where his loud and sneering remarks in public bars about local British security officers caused reports on him to be sent both to MI 5 and the Foreign Office. How he had avoided the sack from the Foreign Office, who by this time were his employers, was quite remarkable.

Maybe Philby thought it would be safer to have Burgess in his own house so that he could to some extent supervise him, or even control his conduct. He took the precaution of warning the British Embassy security officer about Burgess's habits, but said he would keep a close watch on him personally as Burgess was an old friend. What Philby had overlooked was that Americans both in the CIA and the FBI looked askance at such a character as Burgess sharing the home of the very senior British Intelligence officer who was liaising with them.

Throughout the nine months which Burgess spent in Washington, his conduct was as erratic as ever. He aggravated matters by upsetting his colleagues in the Embassy and by baiting the security officer. At home with the Philbys, while he endeared himself to their children by bringing them innumerable presents and spending hours playing with their electric train, his heavy drinking and irregularities worried Aileen Philby. Eventually he was posted back to London.

By this time Philby knew that, though the list of suspects of a traitor within the Foreign Service had been narrowed down to half a dozen people, Donald Maclean was high up on that list. In desperation Philby seems to have suggested the most improbable names as 'personnel worth taking a look at', including at least two men who rose to senior ambassadorships. However time was running out and the Americans were making their own inquiries. Maclean was a prominent suspect not only on account of his own indiscreet conduct on occasions, but because he had served in Washington during a period of leakages of top secret information and had had access to material on nuclear weaponry. He had just been appointed head of the American Department of the Foreign Office in London, and as a precaution certain categories of secret information were being withheld from him while he was under surveillance by MI 5.

It was assumed for a long time that Philby told Burgess all about Maclean being suspected and charged him to warn the young diplomat personally when he returned to London and to arrange for his escape before the net closed in on him. But the truth is rather different. It is unthinkable that Philby would have taken any such action without consulting the Russians

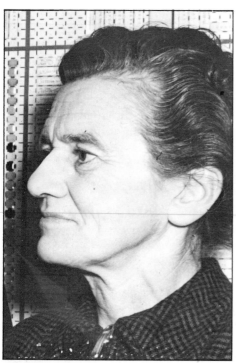

Dame Marjorie Maxse

Sir Stewart Menzies in 1967

Otto John in 1959

James Angleton in 1975

Kim Philby with his mother at her home in Kensington, November 1955

and they would have relied on an agent in London to tip off Maclean. In fact, following instructions from Moscow, a Soviet agent in London was ordered to contact Burgess, telling him to ensure that Maclean speedily left the country as his interrogation by MI 5 was about to take place. For, quite apart from Philby's tip-off, the Russians had been informed by their own mole inside MI 5 that Maclean was about to be interrogated within the next week or ten days.

There is still some controversy as to the identity of the Soviet agent who tipped off Burgess and Maclean. Professor Anthony Blunt, formerly Sir Anthony Blunt, until stripped of his knighthood, and Surveyor of the Queen's pictures was a prime suspect. He had been at Cambridge with Burgess and Maclean and had been recruited along with the former into Soviet Intelligence some years before World War II. During that war he had served both in Military Intelligence and in MI 5. But, since the belated revelation in 1979 that Blunt had been a Soviet agent, he has specifically denied that he tipped off Maclean.

It is now thought that the man who arranged the escape of Burgess and Maclean was a distinguished biographer who died some few years ago. Up to that time Maclean had merely been secretly shadowed and investigated by MI 5 and the Foreign Office's own security people. A stronger character might even have calmly bluffed his way out of trouble, but Maclean had had various nervous breakdowns during his time in the Diplomatic Service. Some of his friends thought he was on the verge of one again. Certainly the Russians must have felt it was wisest to get him out of the country lest he should crack up under interrogation. Burgess called on Maclean at his home at Tatsfield in Surrey on the evening of 25 May 1951, and the pair left for Southampton shortly afterwards. There they boarded the cross-Channel ferry to France, after which all traces of them were lost until they finally surfaced in Moscow.

Geoffrey Patterson, MI 5's man in Washington, was swiftly on the phone to Philby: 'Maclean has fled the country,' he told him. 'That is bad enough, but there is worse to come. The man you had staying with you until recently, Guy Burgess, has gone with him'.

From that moment Philby must have known that Burgess's defection was a devastating blow to his own prospects of promotion. Inevitably somebody would start asking questions about him and, once that started, there was no saying how it would end. Clearly Maclean had been warned by somebody that he was being investigated and equally clearly, or so it seemed, Burgess, though not himself under investigation had decided to go with him. Was this on Soviet orders?

Philby and Maclean hardly knew each other except by reputation. Their paths had never crossed and this fact was regarded by some as being in Philby's favour. Philby was also clever enough to attack the slack and ludicrous security measures in investigating Maclean. He pointed out, with logic entirely on his side, that if Maclean had been a Soviet agent since before the war, then he was already a seasoned operator who would quickly detect that he was being secretly investigated. In any event he must have been alerted to the fact that he was probably under surveillance once he realised that certain top secret papers were not being circulated to him.

Philby did not have long to wait. Soon he was summoned to London to report to MI 6 headquarters and there informed that Dick Goldsmith White (knighted in 1955) of MI 5 wished to see him personally. Naturally, he was closely questioned about his association with Guy Burgess dating back to the days when they were together at Cambridge.

His colleagues in MI 6 from the chief downwards gave the impression of accepting Philby's story. They were always gleefully eager to accept any story that knocked MI 5, for there was a ridiculous animosity between the two services. They felt Philby had been the victim of circumstance. Their opposite numbers in the newly created CIA did not take such a charitable view. They decided it was quite impossible to have Philby as a liaison officer after what had happened. The atmosphere in Washington was poisoned with mistrust and this could only be dissipated by Philby's removal and the appointment of a new man. However much MI 6 may have wanted to keep Philby on in this post, American pressure for his removal was relentless.

So 'C' reluctantly informed Philby that, though he hated doing this to an old friend, he must ask for his resignation from the Washington post. With the resignation went a golden handshake to the tune of £4,000, paid in instalments. But it was quietly understood that MI 6 had no desire to lose Philby's services and that, though he would have to shed all links with the Foreign Service (he had held such cover titles as First Secretary of Embassy in Turkey while he was MI 6 man there), there would be other opportunities for him. Obviously the plan was that Philby should appear to have cut all links with the Service, while keeping contact with MI 6.

'From the earliest discussions of Maclean's escape, my Soviet colleagues had been mindful that something might go wrong and put me in danger,' Philby stated years later. 'To meet such a possibility, we had elaborated an escape plan for myself, to be put into effect at my discretion in case of extreme urgency.'

Obviously it was decided that there was no need for such a move. While Donald Maclean would almost certainly have broken down under interrogation, Philby never lost his cool. Not even when the inquiry into the Burgess-Maclean affair was opened in 1951 and he came under cross-examination from H. J. P. Milmo who was not only a King's Counsel but had worked for MI 5 during the war. Then came weeks of patient, but relentless interrogation by William Skardon, well known as one of the most efficient and dreaded of all MI 5's investigators.

Unquestionably, MI 5 were convinced that Philby had not told the truth in all respects. But, as he himself said, 'the evidence against me was impressive, but it was not yet conclusive'.

But for some time to come both Philby's British and Russian controllers broke off relations with him. This was normal practice in such a situation on both sides. Philby had never been exactly prudent in his financial affairs and this must have been a worrying period with no worthwhile job in sight. His marital affairs were also in disarray again; he had more or less left Aileen who was largely dependent on her mother for helping to support Kim's children.

For the next few years both the British and Russians regarded Philby with some suspicion. While their ace agent inside the British Secret Service had not betrayed them in those lengthy cross-examinations, the Russians would have been foolish to disregard the possibility of his having done so. Suspicion is a national characteristic of the Russians and has been for centuries. They must have wondered whether he had not made some deal with the British to save his own skin, perhaps even a promise that he could infiltrate Soviet Intelligence on their behalf.

In 1954 there occurred an incident which lends some credence to Soviet suspicions of Philby. Otto John, the head of the West German counter-espionage service, went from West Berlin to East Berlin – by his own account after being drugged by a Soviet agent, but by other accounts as a defector. He escaped back to the West in December 1955, and was tried and sentenced to four years' imprisonment for treasonable falsification. He was released in 1958 after the remainder of his sentence had been suspended. Now the Russians knew that Otto John had arrived in Lisbon in 1943 as an emissary of Admiral Canaris to put forward secret peace feelers on behalf of an anti-Nazi faction in Germany. Philby, then in charge of the Iberian section of MI 6, was able to discredit him and so prevent an earlier ending to the war, something which the Russians did not want and which would have checked their advance into Europe. But he must have been alarmed when in 1944 John defected to the British and offered them his services. The Russians must have worried as to whether Philby connived in this plan. Was this why they kidnapped John in 1954 – to try to find out whether Philby was double-crossing them?

In his autobiography, *I Came Home Twice*, John, who has fought desperately for a retrial of his case, alleged that the Soviet agents kidnapped him solely to determine whether Kim Philby was not, after all, a double-agent betraying the Russians to the British. He maintained that throughout his eighteen months behind the Iron Curtain his interrogators never asked him about his work as head of West German counter-espionage, but that the only subject of interest to his chief interrogator was his former connection with the British Secret Service.

Today Otto John says:

If the British had taken up the German peace feelers in 1944 then I should certainly have made the acquaintance of Philby, who was at that time the senior official in the British Secret Service dealing with Spain and Portugal . . . I told the Russians the truth: all our peace feelers had foundered on the obstinate determination of the British to maintain their treaty obligations towards the Russians. In all my interrogations with Michailov in which he asked for names and contacts in the British Secret Service I never mentioned Philby because I never suspected he was my anonymous adversary. Michailov finally convinced himself that the Soviet Union was not being cheated by a double-crosser in the shape of Philby and that they could rely on him. In this sense Philby – I am now certain – was rehabilitated by me with the Russians without my knowing anything about it.

Significantly, it was shortly after this that Philby had a message of reassurance from the Russians: 'I received, through the most ingenious of routes, a message from my Soviet friends, conjuring me to be of good cheer and presaging an early resumption of relations.'

But if prospects looked less bleak for him on the Russian side, a good deal of embarrassment still awaited him from the British press and some Members of Parliament. Subsequent events did not help him: there was the defection of the Petrovs from Australia and their revelations, especially those about the Russians organising Mrs Maclean's escape with her children from Switzerland in 1953 to rejoin her husband in Moscow. 'I am now convinced,' said Petrov, 'that she knew all about her husband's plan to flee. At any rate she began to play a willing and highly astute part in her own successful disappearance very soon after Donald Maclean passed behind the Iron Curtain.'

This report from Petrov was taken up in the British press. It was followed by a number of stories in various newspapers asking 'Who is the Third Man – the man who tipped off Burgess and Maclean in time to enable them to escape?' The *Daily Express*, without giving away any names, referred to a 'British security officer' in the USA who had had to resign. This was an inaccurate description of Philby, who was never a security officer, but it must have been obvious to him that the press were hot on his trail.

Meanwhile the Foreign Office and their parliamentary spokesmen remained tight-lipped and unhelpful. It was not until 25 January 1954 that at long last a very cautious admission was made that the diplomats were somewhere behind the Iron Curtain.

Colonel Marcus Lipton, a pertinacious Labour MP, questioned Mr Selwyn Lloyd, Minister of State at the Foreign Office, concerning Burgess and Maclean and received this reply: 'If you were to presume they are behind the Iron Curtain, you would probably be right.'

This fatuous reply did not satisfy Colonel Lipton who continued to probe into the mystery of the Third Man's identity. Eventually he was supplied with a name and some details and in due course this name was being whispered among quite a few MPs and journalists: it was that of Kim Philby, who was then living at Crowborough in Sussex. Although he was troubled with newspaper reporters appearing on his doorstep from time to time, he evaded being questioned and at the same time took some comfort from the backing he had from his Secret Service colleagues. They, according to Philby, had been duly impressed that he had made no attempt to escape in the same manner as Burgess and Maclean.

Then, during the premiership of Sir Anthony Eden, Colonel Lipton, using parliamentary privilege, asked the Prime Minister in the House of Commons: 'Have you made up your mind to cover up at all costs the dubious "Third Man" activities of Mr Harold Philby, who was First Secretary at the Washington Embassy a while ago?'

Sir Anthony looked horrified, but made no reply. Philby, of course, could take no action against Lipton because anything said in the House of Commons was not subject to libel. But he challenged the Colonel to repeat what he had said outside the House. His own comment was that the persistent MP had 'shattered my dream of extracting a very large sum from a Beaverbrook newspaper'. Confident that neither his MI 6 friends nor the Foreign Office would let him down, Philby had previously said he had been ready 'to slap a libel suit on the first newspaper to mention his name'.

For days he was practically under siege from journalists while hiding out in his mother's flat. Eventually he prepared a statement and gave a press conference. That statement denied that he was 'the hypothetical Third Man in the Maclean-Burgess case' and Philby sheltered behind the fact that, as a former Government official, 'I am bound by the Official Secrets Act . . . I cannot discuss the Maclean-Burgess affair sensibly without disclosing such information'.

And so he got away with it in the following day's press reports. A few days later Colonel Lipton withdrew his allegations against Philby. Finally, Mr Harold Macmillan, then Foreign Secretary, stated in the House of Commons on 7 November 1955 that, while it was known that Philby had had communist associates during and after his university days and that he had been asked to resign from the Foreign Service,

no evidence has been found to show that he was responsible for warning Burgess or Maclean. While in Government service he carried out his duties ably and conscientiously. I have no reason to conclude that Mr Philby has at any time betrayed the interests of this country, or to identify him with the so-called 'Third Man', if indeed there was one.

Thus at one stroke Philby was given a new lease of life and any plans for an escape to Moscow were once again postponed. The Americans – especially the senior executives of the CIA – were furious that a British Foreign Secretary should seem to have gone out of his way to clear Philby. Of course, Macmillan had to say something, but he gave the unfortunate impression that Philby had simply been asked to resign because he had once had communist associates, thereby making him a martyr. After that it was quite easy for certain people in the British Foreign Office to tout at various newspapers unofficially with the suggestion that 'it would be very nice if you could fit poor old Kim in somewhere in your foreign service'. This phrase was actually used by one of Philby's Foreign Office chums. Ultimately he was given a post as the *Observer*'s Middle East correspondent, based in Beirut.

So, for another seven years, Philby was able to enjoy relative freedom in the Western World. There is little doubt that it was MI 6 and the Foreign Office who pressed for a Middle East appointment. There were obvious reasons for this: Arab world intelligence was of importance to them; Philby's family connections with that part of the world were important and he knew the area. But to what extent did Philby himself suggest such a role for himself? It is unlikely that he did this without Russian approval and, clearly, if escape plans needed to be put into operation in future, it was easier to slip away unnoticed from the Middle East than Europe. Somehow Philby must have been able to convince the hierarchy of MI 6 that he could still be of value to them: he may even have suggested that with his special contacts he could infiltrate the Russian network in the Middle East. It would have been a boldly impudent proposal to make, but subsequent developments suggest something of this sort might have been contemplated.

In any event MI 6 was then in the doldrums again, a state it seems perilously prone to between wars. A series of blunders, culminating in the attempt to send a frogman to dive under the Soviet cruiser *Ordzhonikidze* which ended in the Russians discovering this crudely conceived espionage venture, forced a drastic change in the Secret Service. The Government, who had tolerated this state of affairs for too long, tending to turn a blind eye to what went on in the ranks of MI 5 and MI 6, was at last forced to discuss security matters. After lengthy debates in private it was decided that there was no single member of MI 6 fitted for promotion to the post of 'C'. The tradition of a member of the Armed Forces heading MI 6 was ended, and Sir Dick Goldsmith White, head of MI 5, was appointed as 'C'.

Nothing whatsoever has been revealed of what kind of work Philby did for MI 6 during the period in which he was based in Beirut. He travelled around most of the surrounding Arab territories as a foreign correspondent and no doubt he was able to pass on a fair amount of political gossip. But it is doubtful if the information he supplied amounted to anything particularly valuable, though presumably it was enough to keep MI 6 reasonably content. But, as one ex-MI 6 man who has since retired stated,

Kim was, of course, highly knowledgeable about this part of the world and nobody knew better the sort of intelligence that was required. But, as he must have been under careful scrutiny by the Russians all the time, anything he could give us must have been greatly restricted and of a type which would not compromise Soviet interests. But did someone in MI 6 foolishly imagine that one day Kim could be resurrected as a major agent?

Once again Philby was in the process of discarding wives. When he went to the Middle East he left Aileen at home in Britain with the children, to fend for herself as best she could in reduced financial straits. She was only forty-seven, but the strain of life with Kim had brought her more than once to the verge of a nervous breakdown. Her friends believe that she had begun to suspect that her husband was a Soviet agent. Meanwhile Philby lived in a hotel in Beirut and struck up a close friendship with an American journalist, Sam Brewer, and his wife, Eleanor. Very soon Kim and Eleanor became lovers. From all accounts he drank a great deal, acquired a reputation for petty philandering, yet was highly popular with that normally most censorious of cliques – the British colony overseas. Then in 1957 one of Philby's children returned home to find her mother, Aileen, dead in bed in an empty house. Kim returned for the funeral, cooked the Christmas dinner for his children and, after putting the house up for sale, went back to Beirut.

A cynic would say that in his marital affairs Philby always seems to have been aided by fortuity. His first wife conveniently left London for East Germany, his second died and then, within a few months Eleanor Brewer went back to America and obtained a Mexican divorce. Kim sent her a cable on receiving this news, saying 'Clever Wonderful You Fly Happily Song In Heart Life Is Miraculous Greatest Love Kim'. Curiously, instead of getting married at the British Consulate in Beirut, Philby and Eleanor went to London for the ceremony to be conducted at the Holborn Register Office. On returning to Beirut they gave the impression of being absolutely devoted to each other and Eleanor described Kim as 'a divine husband' who brought her tea on the terrace each morning at breakfast time. Yet all too frequently Philby's drinking bouts ended with Eleanor finding him on the floor in a drunken stupor.

It was almost as though Philby found marriage some kind of escape from the twilight world into which espionage had propelled him. Some secret agents are such loners that they avoid marriage; others use a single marriage partnership as a vital constituent and cover in their career. The Philby policy of repeated marriages was a dangerous one. Supposing his first wife, Litzi, had changed her views after the state of Israel was founded, as many communist Jews did, what damage could she have wrought? Or suppose that Aileen had had a nervous breakdown and had talked too much?

Such questions as these must be in the mind of any double-agent, but for one who has been married three times they could be a constantly recurring nightmare. The strain becomes such that at any time a chance remark or a rash comment may destroy him. Years later a number of their American friends recall remarks of Kim's that could easily have warned them of a communist sympathiser in their midst, had they taken more notice at the time.

28

Philby has admitted that during this time he continued to serve the Soviet Union: Russia's prime need in Middle East intelligence was to form an idea of the intentions of the United States and Britain in that area and as he said, 'for an assessment of such intentions, I was not too badly placed'.

In the past ten years more than one defector from the Soviet Union has informed the CIA that Philby was a valued adviser on Middle East affairs during this period. Positive evidence of Philby's continued activity for the Russians was given by Frantisek August, a veteran of fifteen years' service in the Czechoslovak Intelligence organisation, who defected in 1969.

During my three-year stay in Beirut I had the opportunity to convince myself of the KGB's aggressiveness and ruthlessness in organising subversion in this small country . . . and they emphasised the great assistance they were receiving from Kim Philby, the British defector who fled to Moscow. . . . the KGB controlled in Lebanon a network of sixty recruited agents ranging from a member of the Lebanese Communist Party's Politburo, through agents in Kamal Joumblatt's party . . .

Apart from his work for the *Observer*, Philby also wrote for *The Economist*, this cover providing him with ample reasons for taking an interest in economic policies and developments in the Middle East. At home he was relaxed and happy with Eleanor and the children. Sometimes he would take the latter out sailing, at other off-duty moments he and Eleanor would sit cross-legged on the floor of their apartment, drinking and listening to records. They would talk about the prospect of taking a little house up in the hills behind Beirut where Eleanor could paint and Kim do some writing without the constant interruption of friends dropping in. But this dream never materialised.

Philby's journalistic brief covered the whole of the Middle East so he was able to make forays from Beirut to such diverse places as Baghdad, Bahrain, Tehran, Amman, Damascus and even Cyprus. Occasionally he was visited by his father who by then was living permanently in Riyadh. In September 1960, old St John Philby died and was buried with Moslem rites. By this time Kim was about fifty. His once-handsome face showed signs of dissipation and premature ageing. Each year the strain of life as a double-agent increasingly told on him and the pace of his drinking was stepped up accordingly. Eleanor sensed there was something worrying him, that the drinking had a secret cause which he kept to himself. But she was never able to get him to talk about it.

The first major shock must have been when news reached him that MI 6 had been drastically reorganised at the top and that Sir Dick Goldsmith White, head of MI 5, had been transferred to the post of 'C'. Philby must have guessed that Sir Dick had the gravest doubts about him. In fact when the new 'C' took office he was horrified to learn that Philby was still on the books of MI 6.

From that moment it was probably only a matter of time before Philby's guilt was established beyond all doubt. Sir Dick had always got on well with the Americans, partly perhaps because he had been educated at the universities of Michigan and California as well as in England. The CIA, who had without avail warned MI 6 that Philby was still aiding the Russians, now felt confident that some attention would be paid to their views. They were right, but first Sir Dick needed the co-operation of MI 5 and the kind of positive proof which until then had been lacking. The truth is that, unless one can catch a spy in the very act of handing over material to a foreign agent, it is very difficult to establish his guilt.

One of Kim Philby's regular drinking haunts and where he sometimes met other correspondents was the bar of the Normandy Hotel. It was to this address that he had his letters sent, as mail was not usually delivered to private houses in Beirut. The bar of the Normandy was almost a headquarters for Philby; it was here he met Arabs as well as journalists and members of the British colony. He was also on friendly terms with the barman who not only cashed his cheques and allowed him a certain amount of credit, but provided some of those tit-bits of gossip on which Middle East journalists sometimes have to build their stories.

Suddenly, one day in the Normandy bar, he received his first warning from his Russian colleagues. It started with the barman handing him a sealed envelope, saying, 'This came for you by hand'. The barman later recalled that Philby opened the envelope, took out a small piece of paper and read it. Then he held the paper over an ashtray and burned it until it crumbled into ash. 'I remembered the incident later,' said the barman, 'because it struck me as an odd thing to do. Philby just shrugged his shoulders and said it was an invitation to a party.'

Doubtless Philby was intensely annoyed at having a message from the Russians reach him in this manner. It was an invitation all right – an urgent invitation for him to meet his Soviet 'cut-out' (go-between with the resident Russian Intelligence director). The purpose of this meeting was to warn Philby that a grave situation had developed which could lead to real trouble. Major Anatoli Dolnytsin (his surname has sometimes been spelt Golitsin), a senior KGB officer, had defected to the Americans in Helsinki in December 1961. He had been planning his defection and meticulously preparing reports to take away with him for more than two years. He had had access to the files of the departments of the KGB dealing with all major Western countries, including reports supplied by the Soviet moles in those nations. The Russians now knew that he was in the hands of the CIA interrogators. 'So you had better be prepared to answer some questions from your own people in due course,' warned the 'cut-out'. 'We shall keep a close watch on you and always be in a position to establish easy contact.'

There was every reason for alarm. Although he usually only knew the code names of the moles, Dolnytsin's information was sufficiently detailed for the CIA to track down the identities of these Soviet agents. The danger of the final unmasking of Kim was heightened by the fact that in the previous few years there had been a number of other important defectors from the USSR. The chief of these were Oleg Penkovsky and the mysterious Lieut-Colonel Mikhail Goleniewski, an officer of the Polish Intelligence Service. Both men supplied information to the CIA which confirmed suspicions that Philby was a Soviet agent, but the intelligence which really clinched this came from Dolnytsin.

Possibly by this time the Russians felt that Philby could no longer be much use to them as an agent in the field and that more might be gained by allowing him to be exposed as one of their own men. They had lost a certain amount of face by the defection of Penkovsky and one way of counteracting this could have been by showing that the West also had its spate of top level traitors. For the Russians to allow it to be revealed, perhaps even through a bogus defector, that Philby was their man could conveniently stir up Anglo-American mistrust of one another. Finally, Philby's usefulness as an agent had rapidly diminished in recent years. Then there was the fact that Philby was being watched by CIA agents sent by James Angleton, perhaps the best executive the CIA ever had. Exactly when this American surveillance of Philby began is not clear, but it probably dated to within a year of Kim's arrival in Beirut. Angleton, who in 1960 was chief of the CIA counter-intelligence, had established himself as Kim's most powerful antagonist. The American, who had always maintained close links with the Mossad (the Israeli Intelligence organisation), had had repeated tips from that quarter about Philby's involvement with the Russians, as indeed he had had information about other Britons acting as Soviet agents. He was greatly helped by the fact that all CIA Intelligence operations in Israel were carried out by the Mossad and that, though the CIA had no office or station chief in Tel Aviv, certain officers of the US Embassy co-operated with the Mossad. In theory this entailed an exchange of intelligence between the two sides and in practice this worked rather better than one would have expected.

Since the appointment of Sir Dick White there had been less scope for Philby to find out what was happening in London Intelligence circles. However, he still kept in touch with at least two of his former Intelligence colleagues. Anthony Blunt, for example, has admitted that on one occasion between '1951 and 1956' he had helped Philby get in touch with Russian Intelligence. Another useful clue to his dealings with Kim was provided when he made a statement that he actually met Philby in Beirut in the early 1960s, though he insisted that this was 'entirely by chance and purely social'.

During 1962 it became gradually clear to Philby that, inexorably and inevitably, a net was being drawn around him by a combination of American and British Intelligence executives, while the Russians were offering him a safety net into which to jump. He had to choose between one net and the other. Earlier on Angleton had been – correctly as it turned out – so mistrusting of both MI 5 and MI 6 that he had not passed on intelligence of this nature to the British. But now it was essential to change his tactics as far as Kim was concerned: in other words, the British must be made to realise that he had known for a certainty what they refused to believe for so many years.

Thus both directly and indirectly pressure mounted on Sir Dick White to take some kind of action regarding Philby. Dolnytsin, with American approval, made a secret trip to London in March 1962, arriving in a USAF plane, and heavily disguised even to the extent of wearing a wig. The Americans, fearful of more leakages on the British side, were taking no chances. And it was the information which Dolnytsin personally supplied to Sir Dick and Sir Roger Hollis, head of MI 5, which made it imperative that something should be done about Philby.

But while evidence from a few defectors might be sufficient to sack a man from MI 6, it was still not enough to bring charges against him. To ask Philby back to London for consultations at such a time would be tantamount to alerting him to the fact that he was about to be interrogated again. A few in MI 6 may have believed that it was still possible to 'turn' Philby back to the British fold, but there were others who thought it might be wisest to encourage him to defect to Russia. This would at least save the British from the embarrassment of what to do with him, assuming there was insufficient judical evidence to justify an arrest. There was also another consideration which caused MI 5 and MI 6 to tread cautiously.

Dolnytsin, known to British Intelligence under his CIA code-name of 'Kago', had named six other Soviet penetrations of British Intelligence, including Anthony Blunt. If, through rash handling of the Philby case, this scandal was to be exploited either by the Americans or the Russians, the repercussions could have been tremendous.

As a compromise MI 6 agreed to send one of their senior executives out to Beirut to talk informally to Philby. They chose a man who had known Philby ever since the latter came down from Cambridge in 1933, as well as being fully acquainted with the whole Intelligence set-up in the Middle East. Clearly what was needed, if it was possible, was a thorough, accurate, no-nonsense de-briefing of Philby. The best the British could hope for was to learn the extent of the damage he had created and the names of his Russian contacts. In short, an appeal to him to make a clean breast of things, to tell all he knew, co-operate with his old pals and then . . . 'well, who knows, difficult as it is, something might be salvaged of your career'.

To the uninitiated in the world of Intelligence such an approach might seem singularly self-defeating and inappropriate. The truth is that all Secret Services must seek to 'turn' their opponents when the opportunity presents itself and, in Philby's case, to 'turn' one of their own men who had reneged on them. There were urgent answers to many vital questions which were far more important than whether or not Philby should be prosecuted. How important was Kim to the Russians? Did they regard him as only worth discarding, or were they anxious to pull off a rescue act and bring him into their fold?

One MI 6 executive put it in these words: 'We can present the Russians with Philby as a gift, but we must make sure the gift is poisoned – that is to say, that he doesn't do them any good.' The various options as to what the British could do about Philby were discussed by MI 6's visiting fireman and the SIS station chief in Beirut. The former, who, for the purposes of this narrative, will be called Nicholas, succinctly put it this way:

Kim has done some splendid things during his long service in 'the firm'. We have got to find out how much damage he has done as well, just in case he does a bunk. We must know how he was recruited, what were the reasons for his working for the Russians – ideology, blackmail, money or some perverted love of power. And, above all, we want to know if we can turn him to work against the KGB. And, of course, names.

So the stark issue in this most complex of all espionage games – rather like the more obscure of the Le Carré novels – was whether the best policy was to cling on to Kim Philby in the rather forlorn hope that something might eventually emerge from it, or whether to encourage him to defect, either by threats or some other form of persuasion. But this was, in the opinion of the Americans, time-wasting and unrealistic. James Angleton became very restive at what he regarded as shilly-shallying by the British. The CIA station chief in Beirut had discussed the irksome presence of Philby with Colonel Jalbout, head of the Lebanese Security Service. It was pointed out that the British did not have adequate facilities for keeping Philby under surveillance and that, unofficially, the Americans could do with some co-operation from Lebanese Security in undertaking this task.

From then on Philby was watched not only by the British (very loosely), but by the Americans, Lebanese and the Russians. The Americans had a discreet system of bribery with the Lebanese police so that every street trader, street beggar and others in need of earning small sums of money would report on Philby's movements. While the Russians seemed to contemplate the possibility of Philby defecting to Russia with some equanimity, the Americans were seriously concerned at making sure he did not leave the country.

Meanwhile, desperately, the British sought through various discreet meetings with Kim to make him talk about his involvement with the Russians. But, as far as can be gathered, he gave very little away: the vital information which MI 6 needed was withheld from them. What they required was detailed intelligence on who were the moles still holding positions inside the Foreign Office, MI 6, MI 5, or any other vital branch of the British Establishment. They had a number of leads from Soviet defec-

Kim Philby at a press conference in his mother's house, November 1955

Eleanor Philby in Beirut shortly after Kim's disappearance

Kim Philby and Melinda Maclean (formerly married to Donald Maclean) in the woods outside Moscow

Kim on holiday at a Black Sea resort with his fourth wife, Nina

tors, but much more confirmatory evidence was wanted. This Philby did not give them.

Meanwhile he received disturbing news from his Soviet contact. A CIA hit-man had been sent to Beirut from the USA with the express purpose of discreetly bumping off Philby and disposing of his body in Beirut harbour. Instinctively, Kim knew the Russian was speaking the truth because he had already observed that he was being shadowed by a strange American he had not seen before. And his barman contact had told him that the American had been asking questions about him.

Then on the morning of 23 January 1962, the telephone rang at the Philbys' apartment in Beirut. Would Kim call round at the British Embassy? No, he replied, it was impossible that day: he had a deadline to catch for an important newspaper despatch to London. Almost abruptly he rang off. Later his wife, Eleanor, recalled that Kim had been acting very strangely for some days.

I knew that something was going on between him and Nicholas and that somehow it was very serious. And I had heard that Nicholas was coming back to Beirut in January. I was terribly afraid, but I didn't know why. I don't think Kim realised what I was going through. A perfect marriage was falling to pieces because Kim was constantly drunk. He must have been under great strain.

After that fatal telephone call Philby went out to meet his Soviet contact. He related how the Embassy had asked him to call round. Both men agreed that it was too risky for Kim to go to the Embassy. The British might still be hoping he would play along with them; on the other hand it might be a plot to persuade him to return to England. With the British using enticement and the Americans employing a hit-man, Philby and his Russian contact agreed that this was the moment to get out of Beirut. Kim returned home, did some typing and then told Eleanor he was going to the Normandy to collect his mail and to have a few drinks and, on the way, to send a cable via the Post Office.

'Don't be late,' she urged him. 'We have a dinner party at eight o'clock.'

But Kim did not return. Eleanor went along to the party on her own, saying that her husband would follow later. The party was being given by Hugh Balfour Paul, a British diplomat in Beirut, and his wife. Others present on that occasion included both American and British guests, one of them an MI 6 man. When hours passed and there was no sign of Kim, a discreet telephone call was put through to Colonel Jalbout of Lebanese Security.

There are still arguments as to just how Kim Philby slipped out of Lebanon and made his way to Russia. There were many routes he could have taken, either by sea from Beirut harbour or by the lengthy land route via Syria and Turkey and then across the border to the USSR. Philby himself has kept silent on the subject, but in his book, *My Silent War*, he mentions that 'dozens of people make illegal crossings of the Lebanese frontiers monthly; only a few are brought to book'. Certainly Philby told one of his children that he arrived in Moscow with his feet heavily bruised from a long and difficult walk, and from this a story was built up of Philby being driven to the Syrian border in a Turkish truck and having forged Turkish papers. But he has also told one of his sons that he escaped by ship from Beirut. And this is indeed the route which is confirmed from independent sources, both American and Lebanese.

From such evidence it is possible to reconstruct the likeliest route by which Philby left Beirut. One must assume that in such circumstances the safest and the quickest means would be employed. The facts seem to bear this out. At any rate, within four days Philby was in Moscow. The probability is that he once again met his Soviet contact, was hidden in the boot of a large black car and driven to the quay where he dismounted and swiftly ran up the gangway to a Soviet freighter named the *Dalmatova*. Long afterwards it was learned that this ship, registered at Odessa, sailed at short notice without loading the cargo for which she had called at Beirut. In the meantime a Russian seaman was picked up on the quayside by the Lebanese police. He was without identification papers and he claimed he was a member of the *Dalmatova's* crew. Yet the ship's log showed that the ship had a full complement when she sailed.

There followed a long period of interrogation and keeping him in a 'safe house' right out of sight. It was not until six months later that his arrival in Moscow was announced to the world. Curiously this news made relatively little impact in Britain: perhaps after the unmasking of George Blake and the Vassal affair there was a cynical indifference to traitors. But in the USA there was considerable indignation and a sense of outrage that their warnings over so many years had been so totally ignored. Matters were not helped when stories naming the defector Dolnytsin appeared in British papers in July 1963. What angered both CIA and State Department officials in Washington was that the British had issued a D notice (a governmental notice which invokes a voluntary censorship) stating that a Soviet defector had been in London but that papers should not mention that his name was Anatoli Dolnytsin.

A month later Philby's friend Burgess died in Moscow at the age of fifty-three, alcohol having finally taken its toll. Then in September 1963, Eleanor Philby joined her husband in Russia. Though she claimed that the news of his defection had been a great shock to her, there seems little doubt that she must have suspected this possibility for a very long time. The Russians had been anxious to smuggle her out of Beirut surreptitiously, but in fact she travelled to Russia by BOAC to London and then by Aeroflot to Moscow. Though devoted to Kim, she was never happy in Russia and did not adapt to life there. Within a year she had returned to the USA on a long visit to her daughter. During her absence Kim saw a great deal of Donald

Maclean's wife, Melinda. Quickly sensing a change in the atmosphere, when she returned Eleanor asked Kim what her position was. He replied somewhat sanctimoniously, 'I don't want you to leave. Of course you can stay on.' This was his method of ending their marriage. In May 1965, Eleanor left Moscow for ever. Three years later she was dead.

Philby, so long content to drift from one affair to another, eventually married a red-haired Russian girl, twenty years his junior, who worked as an interpreter at Moscow's Scientific Institute. They live in a spacious four-room flat off Gorky Street. The Soviet Union appears to have treated him handsomely, giving him Russian citizenship, the Order of the Red Banner and a generous pension. In his public utterances he sticks stolidly to the Soviet line and proclaims unswerving loyalty to Russia. Apart from visits to the ballet and opera, he and his wife spend most of their time at home. His study has some three thousand books, including, so it is said, all the works of P. G. Wodehouse, surely an odd choice for a self-styled Marxist.

In 1967 he told a *Daily Express* correspondent, Roy Blackman, that 'I have no doubt whatever that we are on the right path' and by 'we' he meant the Russians. 'I will live to see a society such as man has never dreamed of . . . I regard myself as wholly and irreversibly English . . . It is not England that fills me with humane contempt, but the other temporary phenomena.'

As to why he decided to defect, on that occasion he added these words: 'It was in 1961 that British Intelligence sent an officer to ask me if I was working for the Russians, and I decided to call it a day. I went to Russia because I felt real danger was closer than ever before.'

In July 1980, the Soviet newspaper *Izvestia* announced that Philby had been awarded the People's Friendship Order, designated for foreigners who have helped Russia. The paper described him as 'a wonderful man who remains at his combat post'; presumably a reference to his role as adviser to the KGB.

2

'The Lion's Mouth'
Alfred Hinds

'I am not decrying English justice as such: it is still evolving and criticism should be constructive. My quarrel is with many of the men who have elected to dispense justice. I believe they have, by the way they dealt with me in so many of my cases, shown themselves guilty, in the broader non-legal sense, of contempt of court.'

ALFRED HINDS

It was a passionate and burning sense of injustice which propelled Alfred Hinds into becoming one of the most remarkable and sensational escapologists of modern times. To many of the present younger generation Alfred Hinds's name probably means little, yet he was one of the folk heroes of the fifties. His cause and his photograph were then as well known as those of Sir Winston Churchill, Marilyn Monroe or Nikita Khrushchev.

Alfred Hinds wanted to be a free man, out of prison and reunited with his wife and children. But the driving force behind his escapes – there were four in all (including one from Borstal) – was simply his desire to prove his innocence. And this was one way of doing it, because publicity earned Hinds overwhelming sympathy among all classes of the community. There is always sympathy for the escapist, even when he is a criminal. When he is desperately anxious to establish the fact that he is not guilty of the crime for which he has been imprisoned, that sympathy wells up into a crusade. And that is exactly what escape became to Alfred Hinds when, during a twelve-year jail sentence, he got away from prison three times.

The late Airey Neave, MP, who was himself a successful escaper from Colditz in World War II, always insisted that one should read all one could about other people's escapes. 'Many escapes are imitations of those which have gone on before,' he said. 'The example of the men and women who get through has often led others to succeed.' This was a precept with which Hinds thoroughly agreed.

It is perhaps hard for the average citizen brought up in a highly respectable environment to appreciate the difficulties faced by those who come from a less respectable one. Once a person has been 'Held for questioning' by the police whether or not a conviction follows, that person is 'Known to the police'. No matter what degree of lawful or unlawful pursuit is followed in latter years, there is, in the eyes of authority, a question mark hanging over him.

The respectable person would argue that all they have to do 'is to keep out of trouble and get a decent job'. But it isn't always like that, as Alfred Hinds found out.

Alfie, as he became known to the public, could not lay claim to 'being brought up in a respectable environment'. His father was a street 'book-maker' in the days before the legalised betting shop came into existence. Running a street bookmaking pitch in those days meant breaking the law in 'co-operation' with the man on the beat. Alfie admits that at the early age of eight his job was to intercept the local policeman on the corner and bung him half a quid on behalf of Alf senior, on the understanding that the copper would not 'nick' anyone on that pitch for illegal betting until the protection acquired by the 'ten bob' had expired.

Occasionally the copper would say to Alfie: 'Tell your dad that I will want someone on Tuesday.' This demand stemmed from the peculiarities of 'The Street Betting Act' of 1906 which upgraded the fines imposed for street betting for each subsequent offence. A first offender normally got a five pound fine, a second offender could easily be fined twenty pounds and a third time fall could result in fifty pounds and imprisonment. It followed that most of the people convicted of street betting were fined a fiver. This was connived at by paying a stooge five pounds, the copper on the beat five pounds and a five pound fine for the consequent first offender 'the stooge'. It follows that Alfie, being an intelligent lad, must have had an unusual view of police integrity. One inviolable principle, however, stuck with Alfie – 'That one kept one's mouth shut'. This principle did not necessarily help him in later times.

Surprisingly he did not openly clash with the law again until he was twenty-two years old. He admits that life, in those days at least, was a fiddle, but what son of a street bookmaker in London could avoid this? He was first convicted in 1939 with his mother and explains this as a recognisable police ploy. If he had agreed to inform on his mother he would not have been convicted. He wouldn't, so he was – as simple as that.

First offenders in those days were not bound over or put on probation, especially those whom the police described as unco-operative, so Alfie went to prison for a short while.

In 1940 he was called up and led a blameless if adventurous Army life until, while on leave, his home was bombed. Alfie did what he could and applied for extra leave. The Army refused it and Alfie took it. It was while he was in the notorious Glass House (the Army detention centre) at Fort Darlend that Alfie's determination to 'keep his mouth shut' again got him into trouble. While working on an outside working party at the camp Alfie saw through the barbed wire two of the prison staff ill-treating another soldier under sentence. The SUS was dead on arrival at the punishment block, and Alfie's works party sergeant brought in the civil police. The

THE LION'S MOUTH

incident was taken up by the media and Alfie as one of the witnesses was released from detention to return to his unit and appear to give evidence. Both suggestions were now anathema to Alfie and he disappeared into civilian life. The company sergeant major and the quartermaster sergeant involved in the killing received eighteen months' and twelve months' imprisonment respectively, but Alfie was not there to give evidence.

On the run, Alfie got a living by carting bomb rubble to airstrips. Having no legitimate petrol allocation for the business, he bought coupons on the black market. Some of these coupons had been stolen from a postal packet in transit. The thief, a Battersea publican with a famous name, was badly wanted by Scotland Yard. Some of the coupons were traced to Alfie. He was offered immunity from prosecution if he would make a statement naming the Battersea publican. Alfie was sent to prison again.

At the end of the war Alfie married his wife Peg and apart from a minor incident in 1946 when he again resented the way the police tried to treat him, he settled down as a reasonably prosperous citizen running his own business, and keeping well out of trouble.

On the evidence of these antecedents Alfie was later to be described by the Lord Chief Justice as a dangerous criminal.

But the reformed criminal, however conscientiously he may live an honest life, comes up against problems from time to time. One is that in any dealings with the police, suspicion and mistrust begin to predominate. And when mistrust clouds one's judgement, trouble can inevitably follow.

So it was with Alfie Hinds. In September 1953, he lived with his wife and children in a bungalow at Wraysbury, a pleasant suburb on the River Thames, not far from Staines. He was running a demolition firm with his brother in Clerkenwell. One September evening Hinds arranged to meet some men at a public house just off Tottenham Court Road in London to discuss buying a carpet. They wanted seventy pounds for the carpet, and if Hinds was prepared to pay them this price and would lend them his Land Rover to drive back to get it, he could have it. Possibly this may have seemed a complicated way of buying a carpet, but Hinds agreed they could borrow his car.

They said they would be back in five minutes, so Hinds went back to the pub to wait for them. However, they did not turn up and Hinds began to worry as to what might have happened. Naturally he was worried about his car, but he was also concerned as to whether the men might have been involved in something illegal and had been arrested with his car in their possession. He had to protect himself, therefore he telephoned the police to say his car was missing. But he made a grave mistake: he did not tell them about the men who had borrowed his car. The reason for this was Alfie's inherent code – 'never get anyone into trouble with the police'.

Several hours later, after he had returned home, the police telephoned to say his car had been found close to where he said he had parked it. He was

41

told to collect it from Tottenham Court Road Police Station the next day.

This Hinds duly did and he was somewhat angry when the police suggested he must have forgotten where he had parked the car. What had happened, as became apparent later in evidence, was that some of the security staff at Maples, the furnishing store, had been stealing carpets over a period and selling these to whoever would buy. The two middle men who had attempted to sell one of these carpets to Alfie had arrived with Alfie's Land Rover to load up one of these carpets when a snag arose. The security staff, not content with stealing the carpets, had found that they had access to the safe keys of the jewellery department. They had planned that weekend to rob the safe, using their keys, but to arrange matters to make the robbery look like the work of professional safe robbers. The head of the security men refused to allow a further carpet to be stolen that night in case something went wrong which might jeopardise the major plan.

This change of plan resulted in one of the security men being detailed to return Alfie's Land Rover to the pub round the corner. However, being unfamiliar with the gears on a Land Rover he had stalled the vehicle in neutral and abandoned it before reaching the pub. This is where the vehicle was later recovered by the police.

A tangled story of confusion, casual behaviour and, above all, that unfortunate error of Hinds's in not telling the police he had lent his car to those men. It was this miscalculation which first made the police suspicious that Hinds was engaged in some crooked deal. No doubt the fact that Hinds had a police record encouraged them to pursue this theory. Three days after the Land Rover incident there had been a £38,000 raid on Maples store in Tottenham Court Road and the police were looking for at least five men suspected of having been involved in this robbery.

Two days after this, police called on Hinds at his home and told him they were making inquiries about the Maples affair and that they suspected he was concerned because his story about losing his car did not ring true. The police, headed by Detective Superintendent Sparks, were from London and Hinds demanded that he should see the Buckinghamshire CID as they were the authority for the neighbourhood in which he lived. Reluctantly the Superintendent agreed to telephone the local CID. Meanwhile he claimed that he had found in Hinds's bungalow some watches which had been stolen from Maples.

Eventually four Buckinghamshire police arrived at the bungalow. 'I told them that Sparks had some jewellery in his pocket which he claimed he'd found in my bungalow,' said Hinds afterwards. 'I told them that it was an absolute lie and that I wanted the place searched from top to bottom, both house and garden.'

Hinds was never charged regarding the watches. Nothing was found as a result of this search, but nevertheless Hinds was taken to Tottenham Court Road Police Station for questioning. Naturally Mrs Hinds was extremely worried as well as being very angry. Alfie kissed her goodbye, told her not to worry and that 'they've nothing on me at all, love'. But that night he was still in the police station. By this time the police were questioning other suspects about the raid at Maples. Then on 28 September Hinds, along with three other men, appeared at Clerkenwell Magistrates' Court, accused of breaking and entering Maples and stealing money and jewellery worth £38,000.

While awaiting trial at Brixton Prison, Hinds had ample time to mull over the incidents which had led to the police charge. In retrospect he could see that his chief error had been not to name the two men who had borrowed his car when he reported it missing. After that it was all too easy for a case to be built up against him on purely circumstantial evidence. The rendezvous with the two men was close to Maples. And, if the police evidence was correct, the watches alleged to have been found in Hinds's bungalow had originally been in the possession of one of these men. Hinds felt sure that somewhere along the line a good deal of other false evidence was being concocted to frame him. He wrote from prison to his MP protesting at the police actions and asking his MP to intervene. The prison authorities, after consulting the police, suppressed his letter.

At that time there had been a number of big robberies in which gelignite had been used by the thieves and it looked as if all of these robberies might have been the work of a gang led by a very dangerous criminal. But in fact the raid at Maples was quite different from the previous robberies: gelignite had only been used on this occasion as a cover for the fact that the thieves had been let into the store by a company employee. Hinds's problem was how he could possibly acquire evidence that he was being framed.

The trial was conducted under the jurisdiction of Lord Goddard, perhaps one of the most formidable judges of modern times. Lord Goddard had been on holiday in the South of France and purposely cut short his holiday to preside at the trial, stating that he considered it to be a case of national importance. Presumably it was his intention to make an example of 'gelignite gangs' as there had been a spate of serious safe blowings by this method. Hinds, naturally, pleaded 'not guilty', but he was soon to hear the most fantastic story of his alleged misdeeds submitted by counsel for the prosecution in his opening address. According to counsel, Hinds had been in Maples on the night of the raid, and there was scientific evidence that in the turn-ups of his trousers had been found mahogany dust from the safe-ballast, while strands of jute, similar to the outer covering of a fuse, had been found in his jacket. Hinds, it was alleged, was one of two men who actually blew the safe.

A forensic expert testified that the dust in Hinds's trousers was 'indistinguishable from the dust taken from the safe-ballast'.

'You examined it, I imagine, microscopically?' inquired Lord Goddard.

The expert agreed that he had. In vain did Hinds break in to exclaim from

43

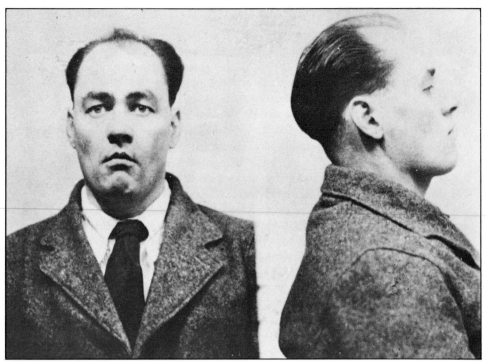

Alfred Hinds in his prison photograph

Bridge Cottage, Greystones, near Dublin where Hinds hid for over 6 months

The bedroom of Bridge Cottage

Alfred Hinds arriving at London airport after his arrest in Dublin on 1 August 1956

the dock 'Didn't anyone tell you I've a thousand feet of mahogany in my garage?' He was silenced by the Lord Chief Justice.

Both Hinds's wife and a neighbour gave evidence on his behalf that he was at home on the night of the raid, but Goddard dismissed this with the comment to the jury that 'it does not follow you will necessarily think Mrs Hinds was right, and you may also think that the evidence of Mr Courridge, who called and said he saw Hinds, should be treated with caution.' Perhaps the most frustrating aspect of the defence was that Alfie was not able to call as a witness the local constable who had actually been talking to Alfie at the time of the robbery some twenty miles away. The constable had a heart attack and died before the trial.

But it was the police evidence which finally clinched the issue against Hinds. Lord Goddard made no real attempt to verify this evidence and showed a marked hostility to Hinds as well as not permitting him to reply to the allegations in detail. 'Alfred George Hinds,' declared Goddard when the jury returned a verdict of guilty, 'you have been convicted of taking part in one of the most serious robberies that has taken place in London for a number of years. Whether you were the ringleader or not, I am not going to determine. I am, however, satisfied that you are a most dangerous criminal and the person responsible for this safe-blowing. The sentence upon you is twelve years' preventive detention.'

The shock of this seemingly harsh sentence was all the worse when one considers what was meted out to the other defendants. Unlike Hinds, they had all pleaded guilty. Two of them received ten-year sentences, another got six years, while the other man, whose evidence had done most to convict Hinds, received a mere twelve months. It was a terrible blow for this happily married man who had tried hard to live down his past and make a respectable and honest living for himself. Though Lord Goddard had not positively named him as the mastermind behind the plot, he had strongly hinted at it and, clearly, it was the aim of the police to suggest that he was.

Hinds felt sure that things could be put right if he appealed. 'If I have nothing else to go on, the judge's handling of the case should be enough to quash the conviction,' he told his wife.

This might have sounded like bravado, but any examination of a verbatim report of the trial reveals only too clearly how biased Goddard had been in his conduct of the trial and how, on two or three occasions, he had appeared to misdirect the jury. After a distinguished career he had been appointed Lord Chief Justice in 1946, a position he held until he retired in 1958. At the time of the trial Goddard was seventy-six and however vigorous and authoritative he might have seemed outwardly, there was a large question mark against some of his judgements. A man of strong prejudices, age did not mellow him and, quite apart from the Hinds case, some other trials which he conducted led to various demands for reforms in the law.

Hinds was sent first of all to Wandsworth Prison and he immediately set

46

about making an appeal against his sentence. Because he considered they had let him down badly Alfie sacked his trial lawyers. He obtained a fresh solicitor who demanded £1000 retaining fee to procure a counsel who would challenge the conduct of the Lord Chief Justice. Alfie paid him the money and saw him no more: the solicitor, an alcoholic, put his head in a gas oven while in a nursing home. Alfie lost most of his trial documents as a result as well as the retaining fee. After discussions with counsel he was able to cite sixteen misdirections on questions of fact by Lord Goddard and six instances of the Lord Chief Justice's failure to put defence claims to the jury. There were also at least two instances of inadmissible evidence and the fact that Hinds had been refused an identification parade. But the appeal was turned down.

The story of the appeal does no credit to the administration of British justice nor to the legal profession as a whole. Hinds had to suffer from touting for extra money by a solicitor's clerk, and – the final ignominy – was that the senior of the three judges at the appeal was none other than Lord Goddard himself. For a Lord Chief Justice to allow himself to be put into such a position was surely not merely an error of judgement, but in effect treating the whole proceedings of an appeal with contempt. Yet, incredibly, Hinds's counsel actually allowed Goddard to begin the hearing of the appeal without a protest. The story that went the rounds of the Inns of Court in that era was that barristers were terrified of Goddard and that he could be markedly vindictive to some of them.

Peg Hinds had no inhibitions. Like many another woman, she had more courage than the man representing her husband. She immediately and loudly insisted that it was totally wrong that the judge, whose conduct of the trial was being criticised, should himself be sitting with the appeal judges. Goddard withdrew. But the other appeal judges swiftly dismissed the submissions of Hinds's counsel who complained afterwards that he had never been so 'abruptly treated'.

Hinds struggled on, indomitable as ever, and determined to fight for justice. He wrote a booklet entitled *The Maples Case* and had a number of copies privately printed. Some of these attracted the interest of members of Parliament. Then Hinds was transferred to Nottingham Prison, where, on account of his talents as a cabinet-maker, he was put to work in the carpenter's shop. He then decided to petition the Home Secretary regarding his case. This he despatched in January 1955. The Home Secretary at that time was Mr David Maxwell Fyfe, later to become Lord Chancellor as Lord Kilmuir. Soon he heard from the Governor of Nottingham Prison that his petition had been rejected, too.

It was then that Hinds seriously devoted his time to seeking a means of escape. He had a remarkable talent for spotting the legal implications in an escape attempt: if ever there was a natural lawyer it was Hinds himself. He decided he wasn't going to *break* out of prison, as that would not help his

47

cause. 'But if I could somehow *walk* out – with no one even knowing I intended to – that could only be construed as "escape from lawful custody", a mere misdemeanour against prison regulations.'

He had made friends in jail with a genial young Cockney named Patsy Fleming who had expressed a wish to make a getaway. In the prison carpentry shop Hinds had been working on the frames of two nine-foot doors. Suddenly he had the idea that these might be used to form a ladder. But, as he quickly discovered, while most prisoners are prepared to chat about escape, few are competent enough to make plans for getting away and only a few more would even bother to escape if they were offered every facility to do so. Which, as Alfred Hinds fully realised, meant that to be a successful escapist one had to be a single-minded loner, patient enough to plan every detail, but determined enough not to be put off by the seemingly insuperable obstacles.

The reason for Hinds wanting to make his getaway in a manner which could not be construed as breaking out was that his prime aim was not so much liberty as to have his conviction quashed. He had already decided that, if he could escape, he would go straight to Ireland where he would proclaim his innocence and try to fight for justice from there. It was much harder to plan a walk out from prison than an actual break out. The law was that if, in the course of getting away, a prisoner attacked or threatened a prison officer, broke through a door or window, or made a key to enable him to slip away, this was technically 'breaking out' and carried a maximum sentence of seven years' imprisonment.

Hinds's method of getting around some of these difficulties was to encourage Patsy Fleming in his efforts to escape and, without revealing his own plan, to get out himself under cover of Fleming's project. It was largely a question of listening to Patsy and the suggestions of others about ways and means, with Hinds pointing out any errors in the planning. This was done in a fairly casual manner, as, while Hinds wanted to take advantage of Patsy's attempts at escape, he did not wish his fellow prisoner to know he intended following in his wake. This might seem devious, but it did in Hinds's own mind exonerate him from the risk of being charged with conspiring with others to escape. But he made sure that his two nine-foot doors could easily be transformed into a ladder.

Patsy had aimed to get away from the prison between seven-thirty and eight-thirty in the evening when most prisoners were out of their cells and in the well of the jail. He had managed to get a key which opened a small door that led down to a coal cellar. The grating over the top of the coal chute was secured by a padlock. To cut the way through, some of the inmates had smuggled a hacksaw from the workshop. Before the getaway was successful there had been a number of dummy runs resulting in frustration, though fortunately not arrest. At last Patsy made his break for it. Hinds waited, impatiently counting the seconds which would mean either success or failure. Patsy got through the door safely and there was a long interval which seemed to indicate that he had managed to wriggle under the flap of the chute.

In fact Patsy had been rather clumsy in his escape and, having failed to force open the bars of a window, had clambered on to a roof and smashed his way through a sky-light. Hinds followed in his path, and, covered in coal dust which he had collected in the cellar, emerged into the prison yard. Opposite him was the prison wall and against this he saw his two door frames clamped together to make a ladder. In a matter of seconds he had climbed this and jumped over the wall.

It was an astonished Patsy who suddenly discovered that Hinds was right behind him. For one moment he thought that the man following him must be a prison officer. Relieved at learning it was only Hinds, Patsy willingly agreed to give him a lift. Patsy had already arranged for friends of his to meet him by car just outside Nottingham.

First of all they had to get clear of Nottingham and the built-up area around it, for they both knew that within minutes the police would be alerted about an escape from the prison. Patsy had arranged through contacts passed out from the prisoners' grapevine for a lorry to stop near the prison to pick him up. He and Hinds swiftly jumped into the back as it came along the road by the prison. After travelling a short distance, the driver stopped, pulled back the tarpaulin and made a space for the two men to hide some way back in the middle of the vehicle between crates of oranges. The lorry was later stopped at a road block, but the police did not make a thorough search. Then some way outside Nottingham the lorry stopped and a car with two friends of Patsy's inside it drew up alongside and rescued them. Hinds was given a hat and a mackintosh to put on over his prison clothes.

Patsy Fleming managed to stay free for three months, after which he was arrested at a garage in the East End of London. Hinds left him almost as soon as they arrived in London.

Next day Mrs Hinds had a message to call at a house in south-east London. There she found Alfred awaiting her. It was not until the following day, 28 November 1955, that the story of his escape hit the headlines in the popular press because Hinds himself made sure that the motive behind his escape was fully publicised. He composed letters to the London evening newspapers explaining his position. They were duly published and made it abundantly clear that, in his own words, 'I would willingly give myself up on being guaranteed a full public inquiry into my case'.

For a brief period after this he moved to Clapham and during this time he occasionally went for a stroll with his wife and children. His daughter was still a tiny baby in her pram, but his six-year-old son trotted alongside. This was an extremely rash thing for Hinds to do, but he felt fairly confident that no one would recognise him. 'For my prison photograph,' he said, 'I had deliberately pulled what Peg used to call "my long face". It made me look a right villain, but nothing like Alfie Hinds.' In the wide open spaces of Clapham Common, he felt they were all relatively safe.

Obviously he could not continue to take such risks. So he set in motion his plan for getting away to Ireland under an assumed name. All that worried him was whether his wife would be able to accept another break in their life subsequent to so brief a reunion. After all, a wife and mother is usually too much of a realist to consider the niceties of whether or not her husband could prove his innocence. But Peggy Hinds proved to be remarkably resilient and understanding.

So, with a bundle of notes from his brother to tide him on his way, and using the name of a friend, Arthur Maffia (surely an odd alias to choose!), Hinds travelled by train to Holyhead. He had no difficulty whatsoever in boarding the ship to Ireland. He then settled himself down on a chair, covered his face with a newspaper and went to sleep until he arrived at Dublin the next morning. There he posed as an English businessman and got himself lodgings.

Once he had settled down in Ireland Hinds spent most of his time looking up books on English law in the Irish National Library. He was determined to acquaint himself with all aspects of the law regarding identification parades, misdirection of juries, perjury, inadmissible evidence and any other points on which he might successfully build a powerful case for proving his innocence. He even made friends with a porter at Trinity College, Dublin, and thereby got permission to attend lectures on English criminal law. Hinds had a natural talent for quickly absorbing the niceties of the law and his fanatical desire to seek justice whetted his appetite for much hard work, including the copying out of long passages of certain books.

He had a very simple means of safe communication with his wife. She rang him regularly at certain specified telephone boxes. One day, six months after his escape, he told her that he was planning to buy a house at Greystones, some seventeen miles away from Dublin, a pleasant little seaside resort in County Wicklow.

'But Alf, however can you manage to do this?' asked his wife.

'Not to worry,' was the reply. 'It's just a cottage and it's tumbling to bits. So I can buy it for a few hundred quid. I can put it in order myself. Just ask my brother, Bert, to send my tools over.'

Then Hinds revealed the rest of his plan. He wanted a place where he could live with Peggy and the children. Once he had carried out repairs to the property, she could come over to Ireland. Indeed, he would come back to Holyhead to meet her and the children.

But the fatal error which Hinds made was to ask for his tools to be sent over. The first batch of tools arrived safely and Hinds, who could turn his hand to anything from carpentry and bricklaying to motor mechanics, set

about putting the cottage in order. From time to time he had arranged to
have funds smuggled out to him and he had managed to beat down the price
of £1,100 for the decaying building to a mere £700. 'I smelt dry rot as soon as
I inspected the place,' he said, 'and I made sure the agents and any other
potential buyer was aware of this.'

Hinds's cover story while he was in Ireland was that he was searching for
caravan sites. He got along remarkably well with the Irish, liked them so
much that he slipped into their manner of speech very easily and soon
acquired an Irish accent. It was then that he decided to dispense with the
name of Maffia and to use the alias of Patrick Joseph Flynn from Belfast.

Work on the cottage had practically finished and Hinds was almost ready
to meet his wife and children when he went along to the Dublin Customs
(using the name of Maffia) to pick up the second consignment of tools. He
presented the consignment note at the Customs counter and was surprised
when the clerk took it away to the back of the office and consulted another
man. Intuitively Hinds sensed that something was wrong and turned round
to make a quick exit. But it was too late: from all directions plain clothes
detectives seemed to be moving in on him.

'Are you Alfred Hinds?' demanded one of them.

Alfred shook his head and insisted he was Arthur Maffia. It was no use, he
was arrested and taken to the police station, searched and held in the
detention room. There he was kept until an English police officer arrived
with a warrant the following day. When Hinds alighted at London Airport
newspaper reporters and television cameras greeted him, but he was taken
straight away to Scotland Yard before being transferred to Pentonville
Prison. He had been free just over eight months.

Hinds maintained that the law demanded that a man arrested on a
warrant should be brought before a magistrate within twenty-four hours.
But it was very quickly apparent that the authorities had no intention of
taking him to court. He was, however, allowed an interview with his wife
and he urged her to get in touch with one or two Members of Parliament
who had shown an interest in his case. By a curious coincidence a Russian
discus thrower, Nina Ponomareva, who had come to London for an
athletics meeting, had just been accused of stealing goods from a West End
store. She had tried to seek refuge in the Soviet Embassy, but the Home
Office ruled that as a warrant had been made out for her arrest, she must by
law appear in court. So Hinds, always quick to find a parallel to his own
case, urged that he should at least have the same rights as a foreigner. The
result was that questions were asked in the House of Commons and eventually a summons, sworn by the Nottingham police, was served on him. He
was then brought before Mr Justice Finnemore on two counts: of breaking
from prison and escaping from lawful custody.

After much argument Hinds was allowed to have his law books so that he
could prepare his own defence. He was not altogether happy about fighting

his own case in open court, but he felt that he stood a fair chance of impressing the jury if only he was allowed to speak long enough and not constantly interrupted by the judge.

Most of his witnesses for the defence were prisoners from Nottingham Jail who insisted that Hinds had simply escaped by following the breach made by Fleming. On the strength of this, Hinds scored his first minor victory by getting the judge to rule that there was no case to answer on the first count of breaching the prison. But he failed to prove that he had never been in *lawful* custody in the first place because his original conviction was obtained by fraud. So he was found guilty of escaping from prison, but received no additional sentence. The judge announced that as the assizes had lasted for eleven days, he would sentence Hinds to eleven days, starting on the first day of the court hearing.

Still determined to pursue his campaign for justice, Hinds also conducted his own appeal against the Nottingham conviction. But, as he himself had feared, this, too, was rejected. Then he petitioned the Home Office and was once more turned down. Undeterred by these three failures, he turned his attention to civil law and considered issuing a writ against the police for not carrying out the terms of the warrant by which he had been brought out of Ireland.

This was a complicated procedure as it involved sending someone to the Recording Office at the Royal Courts of Justice to make sure that the three copies of the writ were in order and all stamped in the right places and also to make a declaration that Hinds was defending himself. It was the ever faithful Peggy who had to undertake these chores; in addition she paid various visits to the British Museum to copy out passages from certain law books. Despite all these difficulties Hinds ultimately brought his case against Inspector Butler – the officer who had arrested him in Eire – as he then was, and the Police Commissioners.

Even then the police tried to stop him from proceeding. When the writ was served the Home Office inquired of the Prison Governor, Malone, how Hinds had been able to sign it. The Governor sent for Hinds and asked for an explanation. Neither he nor the Home Office was satisfied with his statement and some civil servant in the ministry suggested that he must have got his brother to forge his signature. They even went to the length of employing a handwriting expert to try to prove that Hinds's signature was a forgery. When the case came up for hearing, counsel for the Police Commissioners applied for an adjournment in order that the handwriting expert could be called to give evidence in person.

This adjournment proved to be an unexpected bonus for Hinds. Feeling totally frustrated by the time-wasting tactics of the defence counsel and the gradual realisation that his new plea was not going to get him very far, Hinds decided that his best course was to try to escape again. However, if he was to succeed, he needed to do this before the case ended and while he was travelling between prison and the Law Courts. Having escaped once, he knew full well that a very close watch would be kept not only on his every movement, but on his conversations with fellow prisoners.

The adjournment gave him time to think things out and to prepare for the best possible moment for his escape. As to the right place for making his new getaway, Hinds felt sure that this must be somewhere in the precincts of the Law Courts while he was on foot. This was the ideal situation for a new escape because the rule was that, as soon as he entered the Law Courts, his escorts must remove his handcuffs. Altogether he had made three visits to the Law Courts and on the last occasion he had taken special care to make a note of the lay-out of corridors, exits, stairs and cloakrooms. He was determined that he would make his getaway in the cleanest possible manner, that is to say without using violence, or threatening either police or prison officers.

He had noticed that the prison officers and police always used a staff canteen at the Law Courts and that, while there, they always went to a certain lavatory. If he could obtain a key to that lavatory, he thought he could lock his escorts in and escape. While the case was being heard Hinds was being kept in Pentonville Prison and he made the acquaintance of a fellow prisoner who was a locksmith and could probably make him a key to fit the door. Luckily, the locksmith was just about due for release.

Hinds, a meticulous observer, had made a careful mental note of the lock, the key and the door itself. His fellow prisoner agreed to make a key and, what was more, to secure it by tape underneath one of the tables in the staff canteen the day before Hinds was due to return to the Law Courts for his adjourned hearing. If the locksmith could manage to do all this satisfactorily, he was to send Hinds a telegram saying 'Baby boy born', and, if there were any difficulties which had not been forseen by either of them, he was to add the word 'complications' to the message.

This mode of operation might seem extremely complicated for anyone not versed in the arts of escaping from police escorts, but the locksmith friend was in his own way quite a genius. Not only could he make keys, pick locks and make these arts seem easy, but he had a talent for unobtrusively getting in and out of places without attracting undue attention. To ask a man to make a key is one thing, but for him to take the risk, almost immediately after being freed from jail, to go to the staff canteen at the Law Courts and tape a key under one of the tables with prison officers and police all around him is another. Yet the locksmith cheerfully agreed to do this and refused any payment for the risky chore. To understand the astonishing talents and individual initiative of such locksmiths and safe crackers one must remember that quite a few of them were released from jail during World War II to carry on their hazardous profession in enemy territory while wearing the uniform of soliders.

On 25 June 1957, Hinds exchanged his prison garb for his own clothes on

Peg Hinds leaving Pentonville Prison after visiting her husband

the truth. Perhaps it will give fellows an opportunity of showing just how incidents can be misrepresented by our legal system. I'm going to enjoy it.

Meanwhile darling please get the idea out of your head that I look like being a corpse, because believe me you have never seen such a lively looking corpse before. Seriously Pegs just remember that I cannot lose heart because I have you to fight for and the prize just to make you happy again is so much greater than the struggle so I can only see one end to be with you again So Bye darling from your Fyff

xxxxx.

A letter from Alfred Hinds to his wife in 1957

The escape route from the Law Courts as shown in a newspaper feature of the time, which wrongly states that Hinds had an accomplice

the occasion of his return from Pentonville Prison to the Law Courts. Two prison officers escorted him and he was handcuffed to one of them. As luck would have it, neither of the officers had been to the Law Courts previously, so, once his handcuffs were removed inside the precincts of the Courts, Hinds had little difficulty in persuading them to go to the staff canteen.

Hinds had already arranged with the locksmith that the key should be taped on to a table in a certain position in the canteen. One cannot help admiring the way in which Hinds masterminded his escapes down to the smallest detail. He had even provided a tiny sketch map of the canteen lay-out. But that morning Hinds was especially apprehensive because although he had had the telegram saying that a baby boy was born, added to that message were the mystifying words 'Complications but satisfactory'.

What could the complications be? Hinds wondered if perhaps for some reason his fellow conspirator had had to tape the key under a different table. But no, when he put his hand under the scheduled table he felt a parcel fixed on to it with adhesive tape and this he cautiously undid and slipped into his pocket while the prison officers were getting cups of tea.

But when he felt the parcel inside his pocket, instead of the expected key he found a padlock and two keys. 'That was quite a shock,' said Hinds afterwards, and he added, 'I knew some alternative arrangement must have been made. This must have been what he meant by "complications".'

Desperately, his mind racing from one idea to another, Hinds tried to puzzle out the meaning of the padlock as well as the keys. It suddenly dawned on him that somehow his pal, Charlie, must have located the lavatory door and that this padlock was intended in some way to be used on it. Curious as to exactly what had been planned, he managed to race up the stairs to the lavatory ahead of the prison officers. When he got there he saw two screw eyes – one on the door and one on the jamb: 'Their absolute newness and glaring chromium startled me. I realised something must be done immediately because they were so obvious.'

Hinds had the padlock hidden under his mackintosh which hung over his right arm. As the two prison officers came up behind him, he positioned himself so that the brand-new screw eyes would not be spotted, and, with mock politeness, held open the door for them to go in, bowing while doing so. Luckily for Hinds, they went in without demur, and as soon as the second officer was inside the lavatory, he slammed the door shut, clapped the hasp of the padlock through the screw eyes and locked it.

He only had a momentary respite, barely a matter of a few seconds. Even as he was locking the door he felt one of the officers try the handle and call out: 'Hinds, what the hell are you up to?'

He rushed down the stairs, hearing the officers rattling the door and banging on it and shouting for help. Once Hinds reached the 'Bear Garden' – as the waiting-room for solicitors, their clerks and clients is called – he had to modify his haste to a dignified walk until he slipped out of the entrance door into the Strand and made straight for the Temple underground station.

There was one awkward moment as he left the Law Courts. A few yards away he saw his wife staring at him in amazement. She had come to hear his case being tried. Hastily and as unostentatiously as possible he motioned to her to take no notice of him, and hurried on his way. His first destination was Waterloo Station where he had a rendezvous with his brother who was waiting with a car. But though Hinds had engineered an escape that was every bit as brilliant and imaginative as his previous getaway from Nottingham Jail, it was when he came to the latter and seemingly easier part of the venture that he came unstuck. Hinds aimed to go over to Ireland once again, as he felt that, despite his previous arrest there, he was safer in that country and could plan his campaign more effectively from there.

Yet in planning this move, he was taking an enormous risk. The fact that he had escaped to Ireland before meant that as soon as it was known that he had got away again, an immediate alert would be made at London Airport. And, astonishingly for a man who was a careful, indeed meticulous, planner, Hinds had decided to make straight for London Airport. His escape must have been notified to the police within a quarter of an hour of his leaving the Law Courts and by that time messages were being sent far and wide to apprehend him.

His brother had arranged for Hinds to have a lift by car to London Airport. They found they had missed the Dublin plane by a few minutes. This should have been taken as a warning, but after a discussion it was decided that he should travel another hundred and ten miles to Bristol Airport and catch a plane from there. Then his brother committed another error. Booking a single ticket to Dublin in the name of Cottrell, he neglected to pick up the three pounds change due to him. This minor slip on his part drew the attention of the BEA receptionist who, noticing his nervousness, suddenly wondered if he might be a man wanted for the murder of two young children in Bristol. Miss Reed, the twenty-seven-year-old receptionist, eager that a killer of children should be caught, mentioned the presence of Hinds to the manager who promptly rang the police. The police arrived and arrested Alfie's brother believing him to be Alfie. An airport employee had noticed two men together at the airport and as Alfie's brother had no air-ticket in his possession the Dublin plane was delayed while further enquiries were made. Mr Cottrell (Alfie) was detained and charged with 'Helping Alfred Hinds to escape from lawful custody'. Alfie was remanded and taken to the local remand prison. It was some time before the mix-up was sorted out and there were some red faces in the local police.

He was very soon rearrested, as, too, were his brother and the real Anthony John Maffia (whom Hinds had impersonated on his previous trip to Ireland), charged jointly with unlawfully aiding Hinds's escape from prison. When they appeared for trial Miss Reed, the receptionist, in giving evidence, told the judge that she admired Hinds and regretted having reported his presence; she later admitted that if she had known the man she suspected was Hinds, she would not have reported him.

Thus it was that Hinds once again returned to prison, this time to a spontaneous and humorous welcome from his fellow inmates. Those who could get to the prison windows shouted 'Bad luck, Alfie', while those in the cells kept up a chant of

Oh, dear, what can the matter be?
Two screws got locked in the lavatory . . .

Hinds was placed in the prison punishment block, but he still sought every means of publicising his case. He asked to be tried along with his brother and Anthony Maffia, sending a letter to the Director of Public Prosecutions to this effect. He also appealed to the Governor to try to get him a new trial. At one stage he even tried a hunger strike. This lasted for twenty-six days before he was persuaded to give it up. For some few days there was even the unpleasant ordeal of forcible feeding. Meanwhile his brother Bert had been given a twelve month sentence for aiding his escape. An appeal was made against this sentence on the grounds that Bert Hinds had not actually helped his brother until after he had escaped from custody. But this plea was rejected by none other than Lord Goddard in the Court of Criminal Appeal.

Some time after this Hinds was transferred to Chelmsford Prison. It was fairly obvious that the authorities thought he would be safer there, as they suspected that their most difficult prisoner had too many friends among the inmates at Pentonville. As soon as he got to Chelmsford he realised that a very close watch was being kept on him. He was even instructed to keep his head and arms outside the blanket of his bed at night so that the night watchman looking through the spy-hole could make sure it was Hinds in the cell and not a dummy. To make matters worse he had to wear what was known as A-class kit, a regulation prison uniform for maximum security risk prisoners, distinguished by black and white patches on the jacket.

His sole consolation in this period was that an increasing number of Members of Parliament, now drawn from all parties, were beginning to show an interest in his case. But they, too, failed to persuade the Home Office to reopen Hinds's case.

With so tight a watch being kept on him in Chelmsford Prison, Hinds dared not even discuss a possible further escape with his fellow prisoners – at least not at first. Most prisoners would by this time have abandoned any hopes of getting away again. They would have accepted the inevitable and just counted the days to the date of their release. But not Alfred Hinds. Each day he pondered the idea of escape, carefully noting the lay out of the prison and its various store rooms, looking out for any loophole which the routine of the jail offered for tricking the authorities when they were off guard.

Keeping his ears open for any hints of an attempt to escape by another prisoner was one of Hinds's ploys. By learning of any such plan, keeping quiet about it and watching for the right moment, he felt sure he could just possibly slip out under the cover of another man's getaway. At last he overheard hints of just such a plan. One prisoner, serving a seven-year sentence, aimed to slip out through a linen store and over the prison wall. He even suggested to Alfred that they might try this together. But Hinds kept silent on his own secret plans: 'I managed to convince him,' he said, 'that it was far better for him to go it alone . . . I naturally couldn't even hint to him that I was thinking of following him out.'

Once having been consulted on the proposed escape, Hinds was able to advise his fellow prisoner and to point out flaws in his scheme. When the time came he managed to evade the attention of his guards for a few vital minutes. The situation was this: if and when Hinds needed to go from one prison floor to another for any reason, he had to inform his landing officer who would ask him to tell the officer on the floor below to yell up to him and signal with a rattle on his keys the minute he sighted Hinds. This 'handing over' of a prisoner from one guard to another unseen does seem somewhat primitive and open to exploitation by a prisoner as astute as Hinds. But that was the practice during the 1950s in this jail. It did provide the versatile and quick-thinking Hinds with a chance to evolve a means of breaking prison security. On 1 June 1958, he notified his guard that he was moving down to the corridor below. Having done this and managing to avoid meeting the guard on that corridor, he impersonated the latter's call 'One A – Man on, sir' and rattled a tag of laundry keys to imitate the secondary acknowledgement.

Once he had done this and reached the ground floor corridor he was able to slip into the linen store, having seen the escaping prisoner make the same move. Then, following through and noting that other prisoners had allowed his pal Georgie to get away, he asked them to open the hatch for him. There was panic for a moment: it was one thing to help an ordinary prisoner to get away, but quite another to assist the notorious top-security prisoner Alfred Hinds.

But Alfie's determined plea won the day. He was allowed to get through the hatchway on the spur of the moment. In this manner he caught up with the escaping prisoner just as the latter was about to get through the yard to the prison walls. Now there was no drawing back; each was committed to escaping and there was no alternative to their attempting it together. The problem was getting over a twenty-foot wall which had the added impediment of barbed wire on top.

The first attempt was a failure and Hinds fell back on the wrong side of the wall, breaking one of the pebble lenses in his glasses in doing so. With that remarkable code of loyalty which some prisoners develop between one another, his first reaction was to urge his fellow prisoner to get away while

59

he burrowed a hole in a pile of coke and hid in it. But his comrade declined to go without him. So Alfred made one more attempt to scale the wall. Below lay a path leading to a graveyard. Though the drop was a matter of twenty feet, the real problem was that the wall was wider at the bottom than at the top. So Hinds had to push himself away from the wall when he made his drop. In doing so, he fell awkwardly and injured his leg.

However both men managed to get away safely. His comrade went ahead while Hinds dragged himself out of the graveyard, edging from tombstone to tombstone, to keep out of sight. In fact by this time someone outside the prison had spotted them getting over the wall and had raised the alarm. Friends of 'Georgie', the prisoner who had actually planned the escape, had promised him there would be a car waiting for him on a nearby road. They had kept their word and the two prisoners were able to drive off just as a police car came tearing along the road at a great speed.

Despite his painful leg, Hinds insisted on driving the car himself when he learned that his comrade had not driven for more than eight years. He knew that within a few minutes news of their escape would be flashed to police stations all over Essex, so he headed due south and under the River Thames by way of the Blackwall Tunnel. They soon reached the Kent countryside.

There the two men were given shelter and Hinds was hidden in a caravan until his leg injury had mended. Determined to take no risks and keep well away from airports, he made the journey to Ireland by boat, this time from Liverpool to Belfast. To avoid the attention of any plain clothes police who might be keeping a watch on incoming ships, he offered to carry a woman's baby off the ship for her, 'trying to look like the father as much as possible'. Then from Belfast he boarded a slow train to Dublin where he took a flat.

In Ireland Hinds set up a motor business under an assumed name and he remained at liberty for twenty months while the police searched the whole of Europe for him. Funds were very low during this period. Not only had his brother spent some time in prison, but his wife had been forced to sell their bungalow at Wraysbury in order to raise money.

Hinds was as resourceful a businessman as an escapologist and his wife was earning some money for the family by selling stories to the newspapers, while, as 'William Herbert Bishop', he operated quite effectively as a motor car salesman for several months. Then a message came to him in round-about fashion via his brother that a national newspaper was prepared to pay him a substantial sum of money if he would give an interview to one of their reporters. Though there was always a risk that complying with such a request could result in his being back in custody, however careful both he and the reporter might be, Hinds planned a brilliant coup which fooled everyone.

He knew that any such interview would have to be outside the United Kingdom. To give one in any part of Ireland would simply mean alerting the British police to the fact that he was living in that country. It would then only be a matter of time before they tracked him down. But if he could arrange to be interviewed in another country, he could perhaps lay a false trail and persuade the police that he was permanently living there. His preference was for France. Having made complicated plans to get over there from Dublin, he made an application for a passport in his new name. To alter his appearance before he had a passport photograph taken he melted down the plastic of an old pair of dentures, using this to make a set of false teeth that fitted over his own. 'When I put them in,' he said, 'my face became as long as a horse's and completely unrecognisable'.

The meeting with the newspaper reporter took place in Boulogne. Hinds, ever a perfectionist in the arts of deception, had studied French sufficiently in the meantime to pick up and memorise several everyday phrases, enough to give the impression that he could get by in that language. Wearing a beret as well as the set of false teeth, he walked up to the reporter in Boulogne, inquiring *'Cherchez-vous Monsieur Hinds?'*

'Mais, oui,' replied the unsuspecting reporter. *'Je cherche Monsieur Hinds. Est-il ici?'*

Then Hinds revealed his real identity to a flabbergasted journalist. Next day the paper carried the headline: 'I Find Hinds in France'.

Thus Hinds earned himself a substantial fee and at the same time caused police and public to believe he was living permanently in France. Meanwhile he slipped back to Dublin to concentrate on car selling. He had to work hard to make small profits on each deal, as he could not use the contacts he had in Britain and therefore was forced to sell to the trade. Once his wife and children came over to visit him, but on this occasion the police had a tip from an underground informer that Mrs Hinds had boarded a boat at Holyhead. They immediately alerted the Irish police who were awaiting the arrival of the ferry. Hinds, who was watching the passengers coming off the boat from a safe distance, noticed that detectives were on the quayside. His one fear was that his family might not realise the trap they were walking into.

Luckily, there had been an understanding from previous occasions that if there was any indication of trouble at any time when they were going to have one of their secret meetings, Mrs Hinds was to keep her hand firmly on the lapel of her coat collar. This time a relieved Hinds saw that both his wife and his brother were walking off the boat with their hands on their collars. Hinds had arranged for the family to rendezvous with him at an address at Greystones and not at his new flat in Dublin. By judicious telephone messages and other ruses, he put the Irish police on a false trail and eventually picked up the family and brought them in safety to his home. There he surprised the family with a small Christmas tree laden with presents. It was the happiest holiday they had spent for some years. Later that year in Ireland the whole family spent six weeks together – this time for a summer holiday.

Lord Chief Justice Goddard

Aerial view of Chelmsford Prison showing Hinds's escape

The police questioning motorists on the roads from Chelmsford after Hinds's jail break in June 1958

Sooner or later the risks of car trading alone were sufficient to bring about Hinds's capture. In February 1960, Hinds was charged with car smuggling offences in the name of William Herbert Bishop. This soon resulted in his being identified as Alfred Hinds: his fingerprints gave him away. For the smuggling offences he received a six-month sentence plus a fine of £400. In due course he was returned to Chelmsford Prison and the following day was charged with escaping from that jail before a Chelmsford magistrate. Remanded in custody, Hinds was then removed to Brixton Prison where he had the greatest difficulty in persuading the Governor to give him sufficient writing paper on which he could make notes for his defence. When he was in Ireland he had taken the precaution of obtaining writs against various persons from the Attorney-General downwards and including two prison governors. This curious procedure, Hinds explained afterwards, was to cover every possible eventuality which might help his case. When one prison governor demanded to know what he had done to justify the taking out of a writ, Hinds replied coolly, 'Nothing, as yet, sir. But you might try to stop me from carrying out litigation. Only when would the writ be issued against you.'

The years of publicity surrounding the case of Hinds had given him a great moral advantage against the whole of the Establishment, which he had not possessed in the beginning. MPs, some barristers, sections of the press and many private individuals not only sided with Hinds, but felt that something was wrong with a legal system which could consistently over the years deny a man a chance to prove his innocence. By then Alfred Hinds was the only one of the five men convicted of the Maples robbery still serving a sentence. Using every legal pretext he could find after poring over his law books, Hinds became the first man ever to conduct his own case before the Appeals Committee of the House of Lords. This was in December 1960, some seven years since the police first questioned him on the Maples robbery.

This would have been an ordeal for any man. For Hinds it required courage, determination and the skill to argue his case coherently. An occasion such as this is enveloped in pomp and ceremony and there are various courtesies and legal conventions to comply with. Hinds had learned them all by heart. He was determined not to let this last chance slip through his hands. Alfie had discovered that this means of obtaining justice was still available at common law and used it. However, there has since been an alteration in the law, arising from Alfie's endeavours that will now prevent a prisoner from appearing at the House of Lords in person.

For two and a half hours Hinds addressed their lordships. But it was all to no avail: he was brusquely informed by the Appeals Committee that his application for leave to appeal had been dismissed.

Some time after this Hinds was transferred to Parkhurst Prison in the Isle of Wight to complete his sentence. He still perservered in his efforts to obtain a further hearing, but whenever there appeared to be some slight prospect of a breakthrough, the judiciary's interpretation of the law seemed to thwart him. On the facts alone, he was professionally advised, he had a strong case, but it was on a narrow reading of the law that he was discounted. Altogether he made four appearances before the Appeals Committee of the House of Lords.

Then came a quite unexpected stroke of luck. His old adversary, Detective Superintendent Sparks, who had been instrumental in arresting Hinds in the Maples robbery case, retired from the police force. No doubt he felt sure that Hinds had been totally silenced by the instrument of the law and that he was safe to say whatever he liked about the man he had helped to send down for a twelve year stretch. But he was very foolish not to have taken more notice of Hinds's knowledge of the law and his persistency. Sparks wrote an article, published in the *Sunday Pictorial*, claiming that he had outwitted Hinds in his investigation into the Maples affair, stressing Hinds's guilt and containing such statements as these:

Hinds is undoubtedly a very clever man in his way. Though he was picked up within three days of the crime, he couldn't bring himself to admit that he had been out-thought by the police. . . I do not propose to go into details of Alfie's escapes from Nottingham and Chelmsford Prisons, or his constant bleatings against me personally. The jury found him guilty – a verdict later upheld elsewhere – and I think it is a pity that Alfie did not take his medicine manfully . . .

Now there could be no disputing the fact that Hinds had been convicted, but to go out of the way to claim that his pleas of innocence were bogus was quite another matter. A legal quibble? Well, yes, in the ordinary way this is about all it would amount to. But Hinds's firm contention was that not only was he innocent of the crime for which he had been convicted, but that Superintendent Sparks *knew that he was innocent*. And, of course, if Hinds could prove this, then he had a clear case for libel against Sparks.

Even then there were attempts to stop Hinds from bringing a case. The Prison Governor informed him that the Home Office had not given him permission to do so.

'I don't need their permission,' replied Hinds. 'I have a common law right to bring my action.'

Even then he had some difficulty in pursuing the matter and all sorts of obstructions were put in his way. Finally a compromise was made that if Alfie consented to employ a solicitor instead of litigating in person he would be allowed to carry on. Alfie chose a local Isle of Wight solicitor and is on record as saying that this was the first winner he had picked. Eventually a date was set for the case to be heard and Hinds's principal worry was tracing all possible witnesses for his side. This was extremely difficult because of the lapse of time and the fact that one of the men, Gridley, was said to have emigrated to Canada. But eventually, after requesting various adjourn-

Hinds en route to Parkhurst Prison on the Isle of Wight

Detective Superintendent Herbert Sparks (left) with Superintendent Green outside the Law Courts in 1955

Alfred and Peg Hinds in June 1964 outside the Law Courts where his case against Detective Superintendent Sparks was heard

Alfred and Peg Hinds on a homeward-bound tube train after winning the libel case

ments in the hearing, the vital witnesses were tracked down and the case opened at the Law Courts on 24 June 1964 while Hinds was on parole.

Slowly the witnesses under cross-examination told very different stories from those recounted at the Old Bailey when Hinds was sentenced. Gradually the picture of Hinds as a mastermind behind a dangerous gang of robbers began to crumble. There was Frank Martin, the man who had originally borrowed the Land Rover that fatal night seven years previously. At the Old Bailey he would not reveal the identity of the man who helped with the explosives because he did not wish to incriminate him. Now he was prepared to give this man's name because he understood he was dead. It was not Alfred Hinds, as some had hinted, but a man the police knew as 'Monkey' Lewis.

At the original trial two of the prisoners, Nicholls and Williams, had stated that Hinds was not present at the robbery. It was only Gridley who said that he was there. Gridley, who had eventually been traced, went into the witness box. The issue was put to him most succinctly by Mr Justice Edmund Davies:

The allegation made by the plaintiff is that you and Sparks put your heads together and for whatever reason – though the reason is not far to seek – agreed between you that you would go to the Old Bailey and falsely swear that Hinds was present when you knew perfectly well he was never there at all. . . . What have you to say to that, Mr Gridley?

Gridley persisted that he 'wouldn't swear a man's life away', but he had given a poor performance as a witness and Mr Justice Davies's pointed comments to him were not lost on the jury. Every piece of earlier evidence was sifted. Hinds had always maintained that Sweet, the police scientific expert, had omitted to tell the court that soft-wood dust had been found in the turn-ups of his trousers. Now he admitted that this was so. Asked whether this was not a matter of some significance, he made the astonishing reply: 'No, sir . . . what I was looking for was something I could compare with the wood sawdust I found from the safe. That was all I was looking for. I disregarded all the rest.'

In addition to this he agreed with Hinds's counsel that the pieces of fuse found at Maples showed signs of burning, while what had been described as jute strands found on Hinds merely showed signs of heating. These were perhaps complicated technicalities for the jury to understand, but they undoubtedly realised that these were important points which had been omitted from the original evidence on which Hinds was convicted.

Superintendent Sparks had been used to giving evidence to various courts all his life. He was, as counsel had hinted to Hinds, 'a thoroughly professional witness, unlikely to be caught out'. However, Hinds, rightly as it transpired, considered this was a weakness. Sparks, he asserted, was not used to being the defendant in a case. Under pressure he would wilt.

And so it proved. Sparks was asked by counsel whether he had told the Lord Chief Justice that Hinds was the ringleader of the Maples gang.

'Yes,' replied Sparks.

'On what evidence?'

Sparks's reply was somewhat short of convincing: 'Look at his reputation, his record.' During the libel case Hinds, knowing that the defence would make character an issue, sought to show the court that this was a matter that could be in question on both sides. The court was asked to admit into the evidence the facts from the case of Glinski v. Sparks (Chief Superintendent Sparks the current defendant).

Glinski had been arrested and charged by Sparks and found 'Not guilty' on the charge. Thereafter Glinski sued Sparks for 'False imprisonment'. Sparks chose to settle the matter out of court by paying damages and costs to Glinski.

In the libel case Glinski was a willing witness for the plaintiff but Mr Justice Edmund Davies, after hearing the submissions *in camera*, refused to allow the plaintiff permission to bring the evidence that would have challenged the character of Sparks.

Then again Sparks was questioned about his statement that Hinds was 'the most dangerous criminal I have ever met'. Did he still think it was fair and honest and without bias to say this? 'I'd never met him before that case. But following it through,' replied Sparks, 'that was my candid opinion.'

Under further probing, Sparks began to falter, especially when questioned on his article in the *Sunday Pictorial*.

In his summing up, which was scrupulously fair to both sides, Mr Justice Davies said that

'the ultimate issue' was 'had Hinds spoken with the voice of truth, or is he a plausible liar who appears to have attracted wholly unmerited sympathy and support? For the defendant, he has had a long and honourable career in the police force. For him an adverse verdict will mean ruin and the break-up of all things. But in both cases you will throw aside sympathy. Justice alone must be your guide.

Hinds was afraid that these last words might swing the jury against him. The portrait of a police officer facing disgrace after a long and honourable career seemed almost to guarantee their sympathy in his favour. But the last two sentences were really the vital phrases in this summing up. Hinds won his case at last and the jury awarded him damages of £1,300. A few days later the Home Secretary ordered the immediate release of Hinds. But he still wasn't satisfied. His counsel had warned him to be content with the jury's verdict in the libel action. 'Be content with what you have got,' was his advice. 'Don't put your head into the lion's mouth, Mr Hinds.'

Alfred Hinds ignored the warning as he was still anxious to see the original conviction quashed. Once more he took his case to the Court of Criminal Appeal and again the Court decided there were no grounds to upset the original verdict. A curious legal point was made by Lord Parker, the new Lord Chief Justice, in arriving at this decision. It was that while the burden of proof against Hinds in the libel case was less than that presented at the Old Bailey, the explanation for this was that the libel case had come ten years after the original prosecution, the suggestion being that the recollection of witnesses might have been impaired.

Hinds was, of course, bitterly disappointed at the verdict. But in his own mind he was right to put his head in the lion's mouth once more. It is just possible that, if he had stopped pleading for justice after winning the libel case, some unkind people might have suggested that he only wanted a release from prison and some cash. By carrying on with his fight for justice, he was slapping down his critics and demonstrating his own sense of the need to expose some of the incongruous features of the country's judicial system. And in doing that Hinds has become something of a poor man's Hampden in his challenges to the judicial Establishment.

One is glad to know that for many years now he has been happily reunited with his family, and especially with his ever faithful and loyal wife Peg, who gave him so much moral support during those nightmare years in prison and on the run. Today he is living in semi-retirement in Jersey where, as energetic as ever, he is secretary of the Channel Islands Mensa Society and edits its periodical, *Think*. He has also been leading a campaign for establishing a special school for exceptionally bright children in the Islands.

3
'Into Thin Air'
Lord Lucan

'If you withdrew your spirit deep into yourself and out of sight, it couldn't be completely destroyed. But it might go blind in the internal darkness . . .'

ROSS MACDONALD

At ten o'clock on Thursday, 7 November 1974, the chatter in the saloon bar of the Plumber's Arms pub in Lower Belgrave Street, London, was disturbed by the dramatic entrance of an hysterical woman, bleeding from the head and in a state of near collapse.

'Help me! Help me!' she cried. 'I have just escaped from a murderer!' For a few seconds nobody seemed to know what to do or say. Then, bursting into loud sobs, the woman cried: 'My children! He's in the house. He's . . . murdered the nanny. Help me!'

The landlord dashed forward to catch her as she seemed about to fall; then gestured to his wife to help her, while he went to the telephone and dialled 999. Somebody called across to him: 'That's the Countess of Lucan. She lives just across the road.'

Veronica Lucan's home was at 46 Lower Belgrave Street, only thirty yards away. One man left the Plumber's Arms to look at the house; he came back to say it was in almost complete darkness. Within a few minutes an ambulance arrived to take the Countess to St George's Hospital. She told the police who came to her bedside that 'it was my husband who attacked me'.

Two night patrol police officers, Sergeant Donald Baker and Constable Christopher Beddick, went to No. 46 and forced open the front door. At the far end of the hall their torch light revealed fresh blood stains on the wallpaper. At the bottom of the stairs leading to the basement breakfast room was a large pool of blood. Naturally, the police officers' first thought was for the children. They went up two flights of stairs and entered a room in which they found a bedside light on and a bloodstained towel lying across a pillow. Then, in the nursery on the top floor, they saw the two younger Lucan children, George (Lord Bingham), aged seven, and Camilla, aged four, asleep in their beds. Beside them, silent, frightened and seemingly quite bewildered by all that was happening, stood ten-year-old Frances.

Sergeant Baker quietly said 'Hello' and tried to sound as reassuring as possible. 'Where is my mother?' asked Frances.

'She's fine. She'll be back quite soon . . . Now what about getting back into bed and going to sleep?'

He tucked her up and shut the nursery door. Then he and Beddick recalled the ominous pool of blood down below. Together they went down the basement stairs to the dining area which was in darkness except for the light which filtered through the slats of the Venetian blinds. There was some broken crockery on the floor. In the kitchen the light of their torches picked up a light bulb lying on a chair. Sergeant Baker directed his torch towards the ceiling: there was a light fitment but no bulb. Picking up the bulb, he placed it in the fitment and the light came on.

Then, turning into the breakfast room, the officers saw what appeared to be a United States mail bag from which blood had seeped through. The top of the bag was folded over, but the cord was not pulled. When Sergeant Baker opened the bag he saw inside the body of a young woman with black tights on her legs. He felt for her pulse and decided she was dead. An immediate call for assistance was put through to Gerald Road Police Station. Two CID officers, Detective Sergeant Graham Forsyth and Detective Constable Nigel Stewart, soon arrived at No. 46.

It did not take long to establish that the body in the sack was that of the Lucan family nanny, Sandra Eleanor Rivett, an attractive twenty-nine-year-old, who had been married to a Merchant Navy seaman, but had separated from her husband in April that same year. She had not been with the Lucan family very long, but all who knew her testified to the fact that she was very fond of children and liked her post at No. 46.

The police surgeon was called and he certified that Sandra Rivett had died as a result of multiple head wounds. He thought death must have occurred within the past sixty to ninety minutes. A piece of lead piping, carefully and somewhat curiously wrapped in Elastoplast, some eight to ten inches long and weighing two and a quarter pounds, had been found nearby in a cloakroom. It was bloodstained and therefore assumed to be the murder weapon.

About the same time that night the Dowager Lady Lucan, mother of the present Lord Lucan, received a telephone call from her son when she returned to her flat after attending a meeting. Later she stated that she was 'not positive about the time, but it was about ten o'clock'. She did not hear any call-box bleeps. Her son told her there had been 'a terrible catastrophe at No. 46' and that 'Veronica was hurt and I want you to collect the children as quickly as possible. He also said the nanny was hurt, and I asked whether she was badly hurt, and he said "I think so".'

The Dowager Countess lost no time in getting round to No. 46 where she was informed by the police that the nanny was dead and that her daughter-in-law had been attacked and was in hospital. 'I knew something was wrong,' she told the police, 'because John [Lord Lucan] telephoned me a short while ago and told me to come here.'

The Countess, accompanied by a police officer, then took the three children to her flat in St John's Wood. Later – 'it must have been well after midnight,' she said – there was a second telephone call from her son. She was able to reassure him that the children were safely in bed.

He replied 'That's all right' and I asked him what he was intending to do and got nowhere. I also said the police were with me and would he like to speak to them. He hesitated and then said: 'No, I don't think I'll speak to them now. I will ring them in the morning and I will ring you too.'

By this time the police were anxious to get in touch with Lord Lucan. Detective Sergeant Forsyth walked to No. 5 Eaton Row, Lord Lucan's mews cottage around the corner from the family home. Lights were on, but there was no reply when he rang the bell and knocked on the door. So he borrowed a ladder and broke in through an upstairs window. There was nobody in the cottage. Later it transpired that Lord Lucan had let this address to a friend and that his real residence was in the basement of 72a Elizabeth Street.

Later the Dowager Lady Lucan recalled that in the first telephone call from her son he had said he was passing No. 46 and saw a fight going on in the basement. But here the evidence seemed to be somewhat confused as to whether Lord Lucan had been passing the house, saw a fight and went in to investigate, or whether he had actually gone in and interrupted a fight which was going on. It was difficult to assess what he really meant as at the time he sounded in 'a highly shocked condition'.

By now the police had formed the opinion that a murder had been committed and that Lord Lucan, if not a positive suspect, was at least a vital witness whom they must contact speedily. The man who took charge of the investigation was Detective Superintendent Roy Ranson, a highly experienced ex-Flying Squad officer in charge of an area covering Whitehall, Buckingham Palace and Westminster. He had recently been working on an attempted kidnapping of Princess Anne and the missing tax papers of the then Prime Minister, Harold Wilson. Together with the pathologist, Professor Keith Simpson, and other detectives, he worked through the night on the case. At six o'clock the following morning Veronica Lucan was interviewed by the police in St George's Hospital where she was suffering from severe shock and seven scalp wounds. All that day Ranson waited at Gerald Road Police Station for Lord Lucan to contact him as his mother had said he would.

By the end of that day there was no news of Lord Lucan. But on the Saturday morning, 9 November, William Shand-Kydd, a company director who was married to Lady Lucan's sister, Christina, received two letters from the Earl. Both were post-marked Uckfield, Sussex, and there were bloodstains on the envelopes. The first letter addressed to 'Dear Bill' was concerned with financial matters, specifically the auction of some family silver which Lucan had given to Christies three months previously: 'There is going to be a sale at Christies which will rectify the bank overdraft. . . the other creditors can get lost for the time being'.

The longer letter referred to events at No. 46:

The most ghastly circumstances arose tonight, which I have briefly described to my mother when I interrupted the fight at Lower Belgrave Street and the man left. Veronica accused me of having hired him. I took her upstairs and sent Frances up to bed and tried to clean her up. She lay doggo for a bit and when I went to the bathroom left the house. The circumstantial evidence against me is strong enough in that Veronica will say it was all my doing and I will also lay doggo for a while.

The police hunt for Lucan was now spread over a wide area. Airports were circulated with his description and the fact that the letters had been posted from Uckfield caused inquiries to be made in that area. It was not too difficult to ascertain that he had called at the home of Mr and Mrs Maxwell-Scott, who were old and close friends of Lord Lucan. They lived at Grant Hill, Uckfield.

On Thursday 7 November [stated Mrs Susan Maxwell-Scott], I was at home with my two youngest children and the dog. My husband was in London. After I had had a bath I turned out the light about 11 p.m. I had taken some supper to bed and read a book. The next thing I heard was the front door bell. I was asleep, dozing, I think, but I cannot have been sleeping very heavily or I would not have heard it . . . there was a second, shorter, apologetic little ring, and I thought I had better get up and see who it was.

I went to my bathroom which overlooks the front door, turned on the light and looked out of the window. I saw Lord Lucan standing beneath the window looking up towards me in the light.

Mrs Maxwell-Scott went down to let him in and he apologised for arriving so late.

He looked a little dishevelled. He was fashionably dressed, wearing a light blue polo neck silk shirt, grey flannel trousers and a sleeveless brown pullover, but no coat. I gave him a Scotch and water and while he was sitting down noticed a patch on the right side of his trousers at the hip. I asked what was the matter.

Then, according to Mrs Maxwell-Scott, Lucan told her more or less the same story that he had related to his mother, but in somewhat greater detail. He said he had been 'walking past No. 46, Lower Belgrave Street in the evening on his way home to change for dinner'. Through the blinds of the basement window he saw what he apparently thought was a man attacking Lady Lucan. He had a key to the front door and hurried downstairs to the basement. When he entered the room he slipped in a pool of blood and the man ran off. He did not know who the man was.

Indeed, even his description of the man was vague: all Lucan could say was that he didn't get a full sight of him, but 'he was large'. In describing the basement, he said it was 'ghastly and everywhere was covered with blood'. There was a bundle in the corner which Veronica pointed out to him. He said that his wife was very hysterical and cried out that someone had killed the nanny. Then, in almost the same breath, she accused him of having hired a man to kill her. This, he insisted, was something she frequently accused him of – arranging a contract for someone to kill her.

Mrs Maxwell-Scott then said that Lord Lucan told her he had tried to calm down his wife. He had taken her upstairs and persuaded her to lie down while he got some wet towels to mop up the blood on her. But while he was in the bathroom soaking the towels Lady Lucan ran downstairs and out of the house. She was shouting 'Murder! Murder!'

Lord Lucan then told his friend: 'I thought to myself, "I'm not going to stay here with the body in the basement." So I just left and telephoned my mother to fetch the children'. He then tried to telephone Lady Lucan's brother-in-law, Mr Shand-Kydd, but he was out. He had also tried to ring Ian Maxwell-Scott, but failed to get in touch with him.

John [Lucan] told me he'd go to the police in the morning. I tried to persuade him to stay the night, but eventually, about 1.15 a.m., he insisted that he must get back to straighten things out. Those were his exact words, which I took to mean to go to London and the police. When he had finished telling me this he phoned his mother to make sure she'd got the children safe. Then he asked me for some writing paper so he could write to Mr Shand-Kydd. He wrote two letters and we posted them next morning.

Lucan then asked Mrs Maxwell-Scott if she had any sleeping pills, saying he was sure he would have difficulty in sleeping. She gave him four tranquillisers of the Valium variety and he then left in his saloon car. Mrs Maxwell-Scott was the last person positively known to have seen Lord Lucan alive. It was not until forty-eight hours after he had visited her that she contacted the police to give them this information. By that time it was clear that he had not carried out his stated intention of seeing the police. 'I had no reason to go to the police,' she said. Which was indeed true because at that time there was no warrant for Lucan's arrest, nor any formal request for information concerning him.

Uckfield was only some ten miles from the cross-channel port of New-haven and a search for the Earl was made in this area. The first clue to his movements since 7 November came on the afternoon of Sunday 10 November, when a dark blue Ford Corsair car was found abandoned in a quiet Newhaven street. A local policeman recognised it, and as a result of his inquiries it was discovered that a resident had seen the car much earlier

The wedding of Lord and Lady Lucan in November 1963

Lord Lucan at a backgammon tournament in Germany

Some backgammon companions: (centre) Charles Benson 'Scout' for the racing pages of the *Daily Express* and (right) Stephen Raphael

but had not reported it; therefore it was thought that the vehicle must have been abandoned between five a.m. and eight a.m. on 8 November.

The front seats of the car were heavily bloodstained and inside the boot was a piece of lead piping, bound with similar tape to the piping found at the scene of the murder. Fingerprints found on the car's interior driving mirror matched the fingerprints found in Lord Lucan's Elizabeth Street flat. It was discovered that the car belonged to Lucan's friend, Michael Stoop, who had been asked to lend it to him two weeks earlier.

The following day Michael Stoop received a letter from Lucan delivered to the St James's Club in a large white unstamped envelope, the club porter having paid the postage. The letter stated:

My dear Michael,

I have had a traumatic night of unbelievable coincidence. However, I won't bore you with anything or involve you except to say that when you come across my children, which I hope you will, please tell them that you knew me and that all I cared about was them . . . I gave Bill Shand-Kydd an account of what actually happened, but judging by my last effort in court no one, let alone a 67-year-old judge, would believe [sic] – and I no longer care, except that my children should be protected.

Yours ever,

John.

There was some mystery over where this letter was posted from and at what time. Unfortunately Stoop had thrown away the envelope and did not notice the postmark. Detectives regarded the missing envelope as a vital clue and they not only examined all waste-paper baskets and refuse bins at the club, but even checked a rubbish barge going up the Thames. But all to no avail.

The phrases 'please tell my children' and 'I no longer care' in the letter seemed strongly to suggest that Lord Lucan might be contemplating suicide. For that reason the Sussex police launched a widespread search for several days around the Newhaven area. This was difficult because on either side of the port are densely-covered downland and cliffs extending for some miles. Tracker dogs were employed for the search and even the underground passages of an old overgrown ruined fort of the Napoleonic Wars period were inspected.

Newhaven Harbour was also combed by police and frogmen explored the local marina, though their efforts were hampered by bad weather. Later the harbour bed and the River Ouse were searched, especially in a notorious area known as 'The Hole' in which many people had been drowned over the years. Lucan was known to be a competent amateur seaman and power-boat operator, so more than a thousand small craft in the vicinity of Newhaven Harbour were checked by police, as well as boarding-houses and hotels in the area. In 1962 the Cresta Marina had opened its first yacht marina on the south coast at Newhaven. One of the largest in the country, it can accommodate up to two hundred and fifty boats in deep water moorings and three hundred and fifty boats in the boat park. As a potential escaping point this area offered great possibilities.

The suicide theory became less tenable when no body was discovered and two trawlermen reported seeing a man very like Lord Lucan walking along the pier where their boats were moored on the Friday morning. One of them said 'he was a distinguished looking gentleman . . . He stuck out like a sore thumb because during the winter you only see fishermen there. He had a moustache and later I recognised him easily from the photographs in the paper.'

Police checked all cross-channel ferries, but there was still no evidence that Lucan had been a passenger on any Newhaven–Dieppe crossing between early Friday morning and Sunday when the car was found. Nor were there any reports of his having been seen at airports or other seaports. The Earl had vanished. But whether into the undergrowth of the South Downs, there to commit suicide, or by hiding somewhere in Britain, or managing to escape overseas, was a question which still occupies the minds of police forces all over the world at the time of writing.

On 12 November, following discussions with representatives of the Director of Public Prosecutions and with forensic scientists, Detective Superintendent Ranson applied for and was granted warrants for the arrest of Lord Lucan, alleging that he was the murderer of Sandra Rivett and the attempted murderer of Lady Lucan. At the same time Scotland Yard alerted Interpol to arrest 'Richard John Bingham, seventh Earl of Lucan, Extradition proceedings will follow.'

The seventh Earl of Lucan came from a family steeped in aristocratic and military tradition. Born on 18 December 1934, he was educated at Eton and served as a lieutenant in the Coldstream Guards, thus following in the path of his distinguished great-great-grandfather, the British Field Marshal who gave the order at Balaclava which resulted in the disaster to the Light Brigade. John Bingham was said to be particularly sensitive on the subject of Balaclava; yet he need not have been because, although his ancester was blamed for his action by Lord Raglan and recalled home, he was not generally regarded as responsible for the blunder.

Young Bingham was in many respects, both visually and mentally, a throw-back to the Balaclava era, an impression which was accentuated by that Victorian-style Guards officer moustache which he latterly affected as well as by his forthright right-wing opinions. A fellow Etonian said of him, 'You could almost picture Lucan leading the charge of the Light Brigade . . . he belonged to the period much more than his parents'.

Certainly the seventh Earl bore a remarkable resemblance to his great-great-grandfather and he was immensely proud of his uncle, that illustrious warrior of World War II, Field Marshal Earl Alexander of Tunis. In some ways, too, he echoed the opinions of yet another of the Binghams, Lieutenant-Colonel Ralph Bingham, who in 1939 wrote to *The Times* that

the middle, lower middle and working classes are now receiving the King's commission. These classes, unlike the old aristocratic and feudal classes who led the old Army, have never had 'their people' to consider. They have never had anyone to think of but themselves. This aspect of life is completely new to them and they have very largely fallen down on it in their capacity as Army officers.

As a result of this outburst the Colonel was dismissed from his post as commanding officer of the 168 Officer Cadet Training Unit.

But perhaps the real reason for Lord Lucan's right-wing views was in reaction against the opinions and life style of his parents. For the sixth Earl and his Countess were set in a different mould. Both of them were very much in favour of learning the 'reason why' whereas their ancestors would merely 'do and die'. Having won the MC in World War I, the sixth Earl became a Socialist and held office in the Attlee Government as well as being a Labour Whip in the House of Lords. One of Lord Lucan's resentments against his father was that the sixth Earl declined on principle to take any action to avoid death duties. His mother, too, was an active member of the Labour Party and held quite determined Socialist views.

Yet while this may be one explanation of Lord Lucan's seeming swing to the right, it was not altogether the answer. His father had died in 1964, but he had remained on good, even close terms with his mother, as will be seen by the fact that he telephoned her twice on the fatal night of Sandra Rivett's murder. There was a certain meretricious romantic aura about him and one which was almost certainly engendered, albeit subconsciously, by his friends. Somehow he seemed to be living out the depressing picture of an aristocrat in decline, a caricature of the eighteenth-century club gambler who sought a refuge from the unpleasant mundane world of today.

Lucan's sojourn at Eton was not particularly distinguished. He was regarded as an 'average character, with slightly above average intelligence'. When commissioned in the Coldstream Guards, he was selected for the Army bobsleigh team. His other recreation during this period seemed to be racing power-boats. Lady Lucan later testified that he had had two power-boats which he kept on the River Hamble in Hampshire: 'One sank, and a later one he had hit the quay'.

When he left the Army, though still remaining on the Reserve List of officers, Lucan became a management trainee in a merchant bank in 1960, earning a mere £500 a year. But both his colleagues and friends appear to have agreed that merchant banking was not at all his *métier*. It is perhaps significant that nobody suggested what his *métier* really was other than gambling and living the life of a *grand seigneur*. One or two of his friends who shared his somewhat anachronistic view of the aristocracy have said that he was 'a born leader of men' and that in a national crisis he would 'come into his own and surprise everyone'. Maybe, but there were few signs of this. His personal world was a narrow one, as also was his daily routine: he had no contacts whatsoever with the cultural or political spheres, even though he professed the most extreme right-wing views at times. But as often as not these were uttered to shock rather than to express any serious political opinions.

His banking career did not progress for long: as far as Lucan was concerned it was a dead end. Soon he became known as a professional gambler. It was after a surprise win of £20,000 at *chemin de fer* in the early sixties that he took up gambling seriously. His daily routine started with a call at the St James's Club where he would sip a vodka martini and then on to lunch and more drinks at the Clermont Club in Berkeley Square. That he was in those days a man of rigid habits is perhaps best exemplified by the fact that at the Clermont he would nearly always order the same meal – smoked salmon and lamb cutlets in the winter and smoked salmon and lamb cutlets *en gelée* in the summer. After lunch there would be a game of backgammon after which he would go home for a bath and change of clothes before returning to the club after dinner.

Mostly he dined at the Clermont, although on Fridays he would usually eat at the Mirabelle or some similar exclusive Mayfair restaurant. The afternoon's gambling – playing up to £20 a point at backgammon – could result in wins of a few hundreds in a few hours, but the really serious gambling came at night when, at roulette or *chemin de fer*, players could win or lose £10,000 quite regularly.

It was in this period that his nickname of 'Lucky' Lucan gained currency among his friends. Perhaps some of them went out of their way to encourage the nickname and to use it as a symbol to lure other gamblers. Because although the name stuck, Lucan can hardly be said to have been a successful gambler in the long term. But at the Clermont Club he was, as one wag member put it, 'part of the fittings along with the grand baroque staircase and the painted ceilings. His title, his good looks and his patrician manner were in themselves worth a great deal in good will in attracting the custom of people prepared to play for high stakes.'

The Clermont Club became increasingly a kind of home for Lucan, a place where he could indulge his whims and choose the kind of friends he liked. Sometimes after a night's gambling at this club he would go on to Annabel's for a drink or two, returning home at two or three o'clock in the morning. Apparently he suffered from periodic insomnia. This routine hardly ever varied except that on Mondays and Thursdays he played bridge at the Portland Club in the evenings.

A professional gambler's ability to survive may puzzle the uninitiated who always tend to subscribe to the seemingly logical view that in the long run the gambler must lose, if only on the law of averages. How else would

Lord Lucan and Sir James Goldsmith holidaying in Acapulco in 1973

Lord Lucan with Dominick Elwes

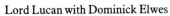

Lady Lucan with her sister Christina Shand-Kydd

Lord Lucan with Annabel Birley (now married to Sir James Goldsmith)

gambling clubs, bookies and casinos prosper? But it is not quite as simple as that. The thoroughly professional gambler knows when to stop, when to consolidate, how to minimise the risks and what systems to apply. He also knows which clubs, institutions and casinos offer him the best prospects – that is to say, just where he will be welcomed as a spectacular regular winner *pour encourager les autres*. Lucan played bridge, backgammon and poker reasonably well. As a gambler, especially after his first lucky break, he was apt to be reckless, but one of his friends, Stephen Raphael, a skilled backgammon player, impressed on the young Earl that, if he wished to survive as a professional gambler, he must show more discipline and concentration.

Naturally, his friends were to a large extent drawn from among the exclusive gambling fraternity of the Clermont Club. They included, besides Raphael, whose wife became godmother to the Lucans' elder daughter, John Aspinall, the founder of the club; Charles Benson, Sir James Goldsmith and Dominick Elwes, all Old Etonians; Ian Maxwell-Scott, who had been a croupier at the Clermont before becoming a director; Michael Stoop, one of London's leading backgammon players; Mark Birley, son of the portrait painter, Sir Oswald Birley, who had launched the club Annabel's, named after his wife; William Shand-Kydd, the millionaire amateur jockey married to Lady Lucan's sister; Daniel Meinertzhagen, son of a merchant banker.

This was very much a man's world from which women were largely excluded. Few women fitted into it and Lady Lucan was certainly not one of them. Before her marriage she was Veronica Mary Duncan, the daughter of the late Major C. M. Duncan and Mrs J. D. Margrie. Her father was killed in a motoring accident when Veronica was a baby; her mother later went to South Africa where she met and subsequently married an ex-RAF officer. Later they returned to England where Mr Margrie became landlord of the Wheatsheaf Hotel at North Walsham in Hampshire. Veronica was educated at a school at Winchester and an art college in Bournemouth. In her late teens she was an attractive, rather serious-faced girl with long fair hair and blue eyes. Like many of her age group she shared a flat with her sister and three other girls in Kensington while working as a secretary.

It was through her sister's marriage to William Shand-Kydd that Veronica met John Bingham, as he then was. They were introduced at the Shand-Kydds' country home in Bedfordshire. In October 1963, they became engaged, and the following month were married at the Church of the Holy Trinity, Brompton. Two months later the sixth Earl of Lucan died and John Bingham succeeded his father. His full official title thereafter was Seventh Earl of Lucan, Baron Lucan of Castlebar, Baron Bingham of Melcombe Bingham and a Baronet of Nova Scotia.

He and Veronica settled down to married life in the house in Lower Belgrave Street. It is difficult to say exactly what they had in common, as they had different backgrounds and contrasting tastes. Few people either at the time or afterwards thought they were suited to one another. More or less from the beginning Lucan went his own way and, at first Veronica seemed content to let him do as he wished. There is, however, no doubt that initially he tried to interest her in gambling (he gave her books on the subject while they were engaged) and she started to go along to the Clermont Club to meet her husband for dinner. Perhaps that was the first fatal step towards the break-up of the marriage, for not only was she obviously unhappy and out of place among the male-orientated Clermont set, but she was ignored into the bargain.

Here again the true picture of the Lucan marriage is masked by the conflicting versions of the pro-Lucan and anti-Lucan factions, both male and female. Lucan's male friends were mainly hostile to his wife, some going so far as to say that 'she had no business to come to the club', while others admitted that when she was there hardly anyone spoke to her. But however things may have turned out in the end, one single anecdote vividly described by Mrs Maxwell-Scott illustrates the fact that at one time Veronica was deeply in love with Lucan. This anecdote is all the more significant in that it comes from a close friend of Lord Lucan and therefore cannot be said to be prejudiced in Lady Lucan's favour.

I remember she told me how she hated the Clermont Club, yet she always felt compelled to go there when John was playing. She hated his other gambling clubs, White's and St James's even more, because once the Clermont was shut John would go on to one of these other clubs to gamble. And women weren't allowed in them. I think Veronica felt some kind of inner compulsion always to be near to her husband. . . . One weekend when they stayed with us and John had a horse running at Newmarket, he'd chartered one of those little aeroplanes and John asked Ian if he'd like to fly to Newmarket. Ian said nothing would induce him to fly in such a small aircraft because he hates flying. I said I'd love to as I think those little planes are such fun.

Veronica who was absolutely terrified of planes, and would become sick with fear at the thought, was told by John to stay with Ian. But she refused and told me: 'No, if John is going to die, I'm going to die with him. We're going to die together. I'm going.'

But gradually the marriage disintegrated. It is easy enough to say the pair were incompatible, but there must have been many other factors in the breakdown which even now would not be possible for a detached observer to discern. Lord Lucan was passionately devoted to his three children and he developed the seemingly irrational view that his wife was not a fit person to look after them. She naturally wanted to retain control of them. The prolonged bickering over the children played havoc with her nerves and caused her bouts of depression. Then in January 1973, Lucan walked out of their home and immediately started a long legal fight for custody of the children. He lost his case and, so his friends declared afterwards, he was never quite the same again: 'It was a devastating body blow when he failed to get control of his children,' said one. 'It seemed to crumple him up. He lost his gambling nerve.'

If this was true it was only because he himself had made a foolish move before his case was settled. In March 1973, Lucan, together with two men, snatched two of his children and their nanny from Green Park. For a few weeks he looked after them in his own flat in Elizabeth Street, while Lady Lucan was beside herself with worry. It is not surprising that in June 1973, he was ordered to return the children to the mother's care. The case had cost him £40,000.

His finances had been suffering over the years. His friend John Aspinall had sold the Clermont Club to Hugh Hefner of the Playboy conglomerate, so that Lucan was no longer the specially privileged client. The 'Free List' of those favoured gambler members who did not have to pay for their lunches was abolished. Personal funds became increasingly in short supply; overdrafts mounted and Lucan began to turn to moneylenders as well as putting up some of the family silver for auction. In short, he was living beyond his means at an increasing rate in a time of inflation.

This was the situation at the time of the murder at No. 46. Lucan was getting further into debt, was drinking quite heavily and had become morose and disgruntled in his attitude to life. Though most of his friends still found him a charming companion, there were a few who felt that he was himself becoming paranoiac in many respects, regarding his children, his wife, the Labour Government, the decline of club life and immigration. On more than one occasion he had hinted that he would make his maiden speech in the House of Lords with a diatribe against immigration.

Some, but not all, of these facts were brought out at the inquest on Sandra Rivett. This opened on 13 November 1974, when Sandra's husband, Roger, gave evidence of identification and there was then an adjournment until 11 December. Yet by that time the police had still not completed their inquiries and there was a further postponement until 10 March 1975. Even then proceedings were delayed until 16 June, at Westminster Coroner's Court.

The tiny red-brick courtroom in Horseferry Road, Westminster, was packed for the first day of the inquest. Lady Lucan stood up in the witness box, dressed in a black coat and white silk dress and cloche hat, calmly and clearly telling her story. The Dowager Countess of Lucan sat at the back of the court, having retained counsel to look after her missing son's interests.

There was an immediate clash between the Dowager's counsel and Lady Lucan's counsel as the former questioned Lady Lucan about her feelings for her husband. Talking of the Lucans' marriage, Mr Michael Eastham, the Dowager's counsel, asked Lady Lucan: 'Your separation was on 7 January 1972. But even before the separation you entertained feelings of hatred against your husband, did you not?'

Mr Coles, Lady Lucan's counsel, protested to the Coroner that he did not see how this could help the inquiries. The Coroner agreed, but Mr Eastham continued: 'You know, although the jury does not know, that the absent Earl is saying in terms (a) that he was not the attacker; and (b) that Lady Lucan was making it look as though he was the attacker. In these circumstances the relationship between the two must be relevant as to whether this is an honest recollection of the witness or is a fabrication.'

Counsel then read out a letter from Lord Lucan, part of which stated: 'V [Veronica] has demonstrated her hatred for me in the past and would do anything to see me accused.'

Lady Lucan was, of course, the chief witness at the inquest. She opened her evidence by describing how on the night of 7 November she had been at home watching television.

My daughter Frances and I were in the bedroom and my other two children and my nanny, Mrs Rivett, were downstairs in the living-room. It was a Thursday. Sandra Rivett normally had her day off on a Thursday, but because her current boy friend was free on this Wednesday she had asked if she could change her day off to go out with him.

At about 8.55 p.m. Mrs Rivett looked into my room and asked if I would like a cup of tea. I accepted the offer and she went off to the kitchen in the basement. I carried on watching television and at about 9.15 I started to worry about where she had got to. I had heard nothing. I decided to go downstairs to find out what had happened.

I went to the ground floor and looked down the stairs leading to the basement. There was no light on at all anywhere. I did not try the light switch. I saw it was dark so I thought she couldn't be down there. I called her name and I heard a noise. The noise of something or somebody in the downstairs cloakroom on the ground floor.

I moved towards the sound and somebody rushed out and hit me on the head. I was standing approximately at the top of the basement stairs. There were about four blows. At the time I was being hit I screamed. No one spoke.

The person who attacked me said 'Shut up'. I recognised the voice of my husband. He thrust three gloved fingers down my throat and we started to fight. I grabbed hold of my husband by his private parts and he moved back. During the fight he attempted to strangle me from the front and gouge out my eyes. We were on the floor.

I sat up sideways on to him and then he desisted. I must have dislodged a metal support of the balustrade on the stairs with my leg in the struggle. I asked my husband if I could have a drink of water. We went into the downstairs cloakroom and I had a drink. There was only hot water available. It was dark.

After this we both went upstairs to my bedroom. My daughter Frances was still in the room. The TV was still on. I said I felt ill and lay on the bed. My husband went to get a towel from the bathroom and came back to look at my injuries. He laid a towel on the pillow and I put my head on it.

My daughter had been sent upstairs and the TV had been switched off as soon as we entered the bedroom. I understood my husband was going to get a cloth to clean up my face. He went into the bathroom. I heard the taps running and I jumped to my feet and ran out of the room and down the stairs.

I ran to the Plumber's Arms pub about thirty yards down the road. There I got help and I was taken to St George's Hospital where I stayed for a few days. I haven't seen my husband since that night.

She added, in response to questions, that on this night her husband had been wearing a sweater, no tie and brown camel trousers.

Detective Sergeant Forsyth stated that he had obtained an order at Bow Street Magistrates' Court under the Bankers' Book Evidence Act to inspect Lord Lucan's accounts at Coutts' Bank, Lloyds, the Midland and National Westminster Banks: they were overdrawn to a total of £14,177.

Most of the other testimony given at the inquest, including that of the Dowager Countess, Mrs Maxwell-Scott and the police merely repeated what has already been told in this narrative. The police had tried to put Lucan's own story to Mrs Maxwell-Scott to the test, that is, to verify whether it was possible for him to have witnessed an attack at No. 46 from outside the house. Detective Chief Inspector Gerring and Detective Inspector Charles Hulls went along to No. 46 to re-create the scene at the time of the murder. Hulls went down to the basement, switched off the light and moved around in the dark at the foot of the stairs where Sandra Rivett was attacked. Gerring told the Coroner's Court that from outside on the pavement all he could see through the slats in the basement venetian blind

was the red glow of the light on the kettle. When the light on the breakfast room table was switched on I could make out the figure of Mr Hulls in the area at the foot of the stairs. Then, only by stooping with my head between two and three feet from the ground, I could make out Mr Hulls' figure.

But he agreed that when the kitchen lights were switched on, he could see Mr Hulls at the foot of the basement stairs.

In effect this established that anyone walking past the house looking through the blinds could only see the kitchen, *not* the breakfast room or the area at the foot of the stairs, and only then when the kitchen lights were switched on. But this did not totally destroy Lucan's story, as was implied.

More pertinent was a question put by the foreman of the jury. He said to the Coroner: 'We have heard nothing at all from Lady Lucan about the nanny being murdered. We heard about her going to the barman at the Plumber's Arms and saying to him: "He has murdered my nanny." But how did she know the nanny had been murdered?'

The Coroner replied that this was 'quite right', but suggested that 'we hear the rest of the evidence and then I hope to be able to satisfy you on that'.

Yet no such satisfaction was in fact given. At the conclusion of the hearing all the Coroner could say to the jury on this aspect of the case was 'You should not speculate as to how it came about that this was said. The difficulty is that in law Lady Lucan is barred from giving evidence other than that concerning assault.'

But the damage had been done: that outcry at the Plumber's Arms was firmly imprinted in the minds of the jury. Perhaps the other evidence which helped convince the jury was that contained in a statement made by ten-year-old Lady Frances Bingham to Woman Detective Sally Bower. The latter read the statement to the Coroner's Court, adding, 'I think she was telling the truth as she saw it. She was quite clear and composed.' Lady Frances' statement largely confirmed what her mother said. It was as follows:

. . . Mummy wondered why Sandra was so long [making tea]. It was before the news came on at 9 p.m. I said I would go downstairs to see what was keeping her, but Mummy said no, she would go down. She left the bedroom door open, but there was no light in the hall. Just after Mummy left the room I heard a scream. It sounded as though it came from a long way away. I thought perhaps the cat had scratched Mummy and she had screamed. I was not frightened. I went to the door and called Mummy, but there was no answer and I left it.

At 9.05 the news was on TV and Daddy and Mummy both walked into the room. Mummy had blood over her face and was crying. Mummy told me to go upstairs. Daddy didn't say anything to me and I said nothing to either of them. I don't know how much blood was on her face. I didn't hear any conversation between Mummy and Daddy. I didn't see any blood on Daddy's clothes. I wondered what had happened, but I didn't ask.

The jury returned a verdict that Sandra Rivett had been murdered by Lord Lucan. In recording this, the Coroner made the comment that it was very rare for a coroner's court to name a person as the jury had done. And the verdict was hotly disputed for several days. Lady Lucan made a statement through her solicitors that she could not say 'that I am pleased or displeased with the verdict. I was only concerned with establishing the facts.' But Lord Lucan's own family were very bitter about the result of the inquiry. The husband of Lord Lucan's sister, the Reverend William Gibbs, insisted that the family 'will investigate what legal steps can be taken to clear Lord Lucan's name. My wife and I are firmly convinced that he is not guilty of murder.'

This was the first case in two hundred years in which a peer of the realm had been involved in murder. The inquest verdict inevitably resulted in the

Sandra Rivett

Sandra Rivett

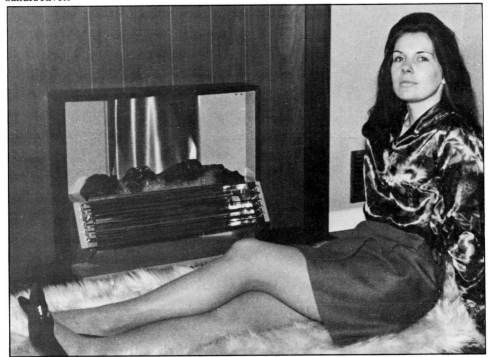

46 Lower Belgrave Street, London, where
Sandra Rivett was murdered

Lord Lucan's mews home in Eaton Row,
Belgravia, where he lived after separating from
his wife

Police divers searching for Lord Lucan in Newhaven harbour

creation of two rival camps – those who were loudly and clearly pronoun-cing his innocence and demanding justice, and those who insisted with equal vehemence that he was guilty. To an objective observer – and in the Lucan case one needs to be extremely objective – one can only say that there is a great deal of evidence to justify both viewpoints.

That he himself escaped from his dilemma is now quite clear. But did he escape through committing suicide, or by disappearing and taking on a new identity? For a long time the official view – always more implied than openly stated – was that he had somehow taken his own life in such a way that nobody would find his body, a final, macabre and defiant gesture. To some extent this official view had been maintained over the years since Lucan's disappearance. Detective Superintendent Ranson stated as recently as November 1978: 'It is over four years. If he were still alive, I feel sure we should have had some hard information by now.'

But the Lucan file remains open and not all the detectives employed on the case share Ranson's view. Some of his friends still cling to the idea that he is alive somewhere in the world, probably under an alias. After the inquest on the murder in June 1975, Mrs Maxwell-Scott told the *News of the World*:

I think it's quite possible that some of John's close and highly influential friends might feel that if he's still alive, he is totally innocent and look after him. However, if that's the case I think they're misguided . . . I'm absolutely convinced because of the knowledge I have of John's temperament, that he's incapable of murder.

Lucan's disappearance remains one of the great puzzles of an age when it is extremely difficult to vanish without trace. Suicide by drowning is a possibility, but most bodies lost off the southern coasts of England get washed up again sooner or later. And in Lucan's case suicide without leaving a note of his intentions seems unlikely unless he wanted to keep people guessing as to whether he was alive or dead. A second search for his body, one that allowed for tides to have shifted the body back landwards, was launched late in November 1974 and no fewer than fourteen divers were employed. There was a report that a man resembling Lucan had been seen by a woman on the cliffs near Peacehaven, but nothing came of it. During the two weeks after his disappearance detectives visited immigration and security officers in Dieppe to seek any information on arrival of passengers or any ferry crossings.

In the first four weeks after the murder the police received reports of no fewer than seventy-four alleged sightings of Lucan, ranging from the swimming baths in Finchley, London, and Kent and Norfolk, to France, the Channel Islands and Cairo. All these leads proved fruitless. The most amusing suggestion put forward was from a humorous ex-convict who claimed that Lucan had joined the police force and in this disguise was on point-duty in Whitehall!

To try to find some clues to Lucan's disappearance the police traced his movements over the previous twenty-four hours. On the day before the murder he had called on a music teacher friend, Caroline Hill, living in Chelsea. Though he did not display his fondness for music to many of his male friends, nevertheless Lucan had taught himself to play Bach. Caroline Hill had taught music to both Lucan and his daughter, Lady Frances.

Later he visited a Curzon Street bookshop and somewhat surprisingly bought a book on shipping millionaires. He spent the evening of the sixth at a buffet supper given by Selim Zilkha, chairman of the Mothercare chain of shops. Later he played bridge at the Clermont Club. It was noted by his friends that he was drinking quite heavily.

Untypically, Lucan was up and about early on the morning of the seventh. He had phoned his lawyers shortly after nine-thirty and at ten-thirty a friend, Andrina Colquhoun, phoned to ask him his plans for that evening. She got the impression that he was in 'somewhat of a muddle and he seemed uncertain as to what he would be doing'. From then until about four p.m. there is no evidence as to where Lucan was. But at the latter hour he was having drinks with a friend, Michael Hicks Beach, discussing an article on gambling that Lucan was writing. He drove Hicks Beach back to the latter's flat in Fulham about seven o'clock. Then he returned to his Elizabeth Street home to change.

At eight-thirty p.m. Lucan telephoned the Clermont to book a table for four for ten-thirty that night. A quarter of an hour later he arrived at the club by car, stopping at the lobby window to ask if any of his friends were there. Then he drove off. Presumably he returned to Elizabeth Street and then went round to No. 46 Lower Belgrave Street. And after that he must have driven to Uckfield and the Maxwell-Scott home. Meanwhile his guests at the Clermont waited for him in vain.

This narrative of Lucan's movements provides no clear clues as to his intentions. It is true that there was a gap of some few hours prior to four p.m. that fatal Thursday, and an accurate account of that period might reveal something significant, otherwise there is no indication of a man planning to flee the country, or disappear. But there is another rather more important gap in the story. Assuming that his car was abandoned in Newhaven between five and eight o'clock on the Friday morning, which the police believe to have been the case, what was Lucan doing between leaving the Maxwell-Scotts at one-fifteen a.m. and five o'clock. It would not have taken him more than half an hour at the most to drive from Uckfield to Newhaven at that time of night.

One explanation could be that Lucan stopped in some quiet place en route – possibly a field – and either had a brief nap, which seems highly improbable, or stopped to think out his next move. Or he could have driven elsewhere and later a fellow conspirator could have taken the car to Newhaven to lay a false trail.

ESCAPE!

His friends maintained a discreet silence. They were bewildered more than anything else by what had happened because, as one of them said:

None of it made sense. I mean if 'Lucky' had wanted to bump off his wife, he would hardly have gone round to No. 46 armed with lead piping like a Bill Sykes type. And he would hardly have bumped off the nanny instead of his wife by mistake and then failed to finish off his wife when he realised what he had done. It just doesn't make sense that he could make such a botch of things. Apart from that the whole affair was out of character.

To which this friend might have added that nor would Lucan have been likely to leave a similar piece of lead piping in his car. Nor, for that matter, is it likely that he would have left the original murder weapon at No. 46. On the other hand it is a fact that on this Thursday night normally Sandra Rivett would have been off duty: he was not to know that this had been changed. So, if he were lying in wait with the murder weapon in the darkness of the basement, having removed the light bulb, he would expect any adult female steps coming down the stairs to be those of his wife and not the nanny. And, as there were no signs of the door to No. 46 having been forced open, and nobody else had a key, who but Lord Lucan could have gained access to the house without ringing the front-door bell? There was just one other slight possibility – that one of Sandra Rivett's male friends had had an extra key cut.

This was extremely unlikely, but it was seized on by some of Lucan's friends. The police had discovered from a list of addresses in her possession that Sandra Rivett had several men friends, though their inquiries among them proved unavailing. A few of the Lucan set actually hired a private detective to try to establish his innocence. An unofficial search was made for the mysterious assailant mentioned by Lucan to Mrs Maxwell-Scott. But if there was a strange assailant, no motive presented itself for killing the nanny. Not only were there no signs of forcible entry, but nothing was stolen and there were no indications of a sexual assault on the unfortunate young woman.

Reluctantly [said one of Lucan's friends] we were forced to contemplate the fact that Lucan had after all mistaken Sandra Rivett for his wife in the darkness of the basement and that this was the reason for the murder. But it was all so clumsy, so out of character, even ridiculous that somehow one couldn't accept that as being the whole truth. Originally, some of us who were close friends of 'Lucky' telephoned one another, and, in effect, we said: What the hell do we do if 'Lucky' suddenly gets in touch with us? After all, he was our friend and we didn't know for certain that he had committed a murder.

His friend John Aspinall has said that 'people were worried about what to do if he turned up . . . Every contingency was looked at.' And there is no doubt that among his clubland friends and some of the gambling fraternity there was a real desire to lend Lucan legitimate help if he needed it, or got in

94

touch with any of them. The police stepped up their hunt for Lucan over a very wide area both in this country and overseas. Various estates of wealthy acquaintances of Lucan's were searched by police using dogs. In mid-November plain clothes police of the Special Patrol Group combed a large part of Belgravia looking for clues, and using two-way radio sets to keep in touch. When they went into private gardens and down basement steps as well as searching public gardens they had some highly indignant reactions from local residents. Eventually the police had to admit that it did not seem that anyone in Britain was knowingly sheltering Lucan. Ranson, referring to the accessibility of Lucan's wide circle of friends, said, 'Well, they aren't exactly queuing up at the police station door to see me. And when they have several addresses it's not the easiest thing to arrange a meeting. If they are reluctant to come here, we go and see them.'

But the police admitted the difficulties involved in a case of this kind. They were not dealing with the usual criminal underworld where help was often provided by informers. Lucan's friends were infuriated when Marcus Lipton, the Labour MP for Lambeth Central, commented that 'it looks as if some people are being a bit snooty. All citizens, whatever their station in life, must be made aware that if they have any knowledge which throws light on a serious crime, the facts should be disclosed to the police,' at the same time hinting that he was raising the matter with the Home Secretary. Mr Charles Benson, Lucan's Old Etonian friend, wrote a letter to *The Times*, refuting Lipton's claim:

As a still close friend of Lord Lucan, could I make my own position clear. As far as I know, all his friends have made themselves available to the police at all times. I personally rang the department concerned on the Friday morning following the murder, giving my name and address, and also offering other names, all of whom were in full agreement. I may add that we were not contacted for some days. Is this obstruction or non-co-operation by us? Could Mr Lipton please identify those whom he believes to be failing in their public duty. If not, would he kindly withdraw his remarks.

There was one discrepancy between the evidence of Lady Lucan and that of her daughter, Lady Frances, which puzzled the police and has never been satisfactorily explained. Lady Lucan insisted that it was 'about nine-fifteen' that she went downstairs to look for Sandra Rivett, whereas her daughter said 'it was before the news on TV at nine p.m.' Almost as baffling was a mysterious telephone call received by a Chelsea friend of Lucan's between ten and ten-thirty on the night of the murder. Three words were spoken and then the voice was cut off: the recipient felt sure that it was Lucan who had called.

If Lucan is still alive, it seems fairly certain that he is living outside Britain. It is quite likely that he did not leave the country by sea, but that he laid a trail to suggest this. He was used to chartering private aircraft for

Lady Lucan leaving the Coroner's Court in Westminster after the verdict
The Dowager Countess of Lucan with Bill Shand-Kydd on their way to the Coroner's Court

Detective Chief Superintendent Roy Ransom

Mrs Susan Maxwell-Scott taking a lunchtime break during the inquest

Roger Rivett, the husband of the murdered nanny

Lady Lucan

Lord Lucan with his son, George, then aged about four

various trips and it is possible that he left the country by this means in the early hours of 8 November, most probably from a private airfield not too far distant from Newhaven. He could even have been taken off from a field within easy reach of Uckfield. France would have been the likeliest destination, as he had friends in that country. Though he had a bank account in Switzerland, that country would have been far too small for him to have remained undiscovered there for long. From all accounts he spoke just enough French to get along as a holidaymaker. In that country he could possibly have been hidden away quite easily.

Those who knew him best doubted whether he could survive in many of the more exotic but remoter parts of the globe where extradition was ruled out. When a telegram arrived at Lucan's Elizabeth Street flat, offering him the use of a house in Haiti (this later turned out to be the first of many hoaxes), John Aspinall commented that 'I know few people less fitted to be a fugitive in Haiti or Brazil. I don't think he has the capacity to adapt.'

Could his friends have been underestimating 'Lucky' Lucan's ability – and perhaps his luck – to survive? If he is still alive, then not only has he managed to obliterate all clues to his whereabouts since he left Uckfield, but he has remained undiscovered for six years, a remarkable feat for anyone as well known as Lucan over a period of such length in modern times.

At the end of November 1974, there was a reported sighting of him at an exclusive party in Cape Town. As Britain had no extradition treaty with South Africa, photographs and personal details of Lucan were forwarded to Cape Town at the request of the Foreign Office. But within twenty-four hours the South African police dismissed the report as unfounded. Notwithstanding this, the Lucan trail, since his disappearance, has frequently led back to the African continent. This may have been partly due to gossip and partly because he was known to have friends in South Africa and Rhodesia. His brother, the Hon. Hugh Bingham, went to South Africa in July 1975, to seek work as a gold prospector.

So thorough was the watch for Lord Lucan in the furthermost parts of the world that, though it did not lead to his arrest, it was a vital factor in preventing the permanent disappearance of yet another Englishman, Mr John Stonehouse, MP and former Postmaster-General, who had vanished from a Miami beach the year before. Interpol had sent out a message to its Australian headquarters in Melbourne regarding Lucan, stressing that he might have entered Australia on an Irish passport. It was because they were on the look-out for Lucan that the suspicions of the Victorian police were aroused by the presence of a man living in Melbourne under two names, Joseph Arthur Markham and Donald Clive Muldoon. Having been taken in for questioning, and after the Australian authorities had checked back with Scotland Yard, Markham alias Muldoon was found to be not Lucan, but John Stonehouse. He was sent back to Britain to face charges of forgery, theft and false pretences.

A week after the Lucan inquest in June 1975, Superintendent Ranson and Detective Chief Inspector Gerring flew to Cherbourg after receiving a message from Interpol. Superintendent Ranson said afterwards that obviously the French police had been convinced that Lucan had been seen and identified, but 'we were pretty sure they were mistaken'. Then came a report that Lucan had undergone plastic surgery and had been smuggled out of the country on a private yacht. A team of police questioned staff at various private clinics throughout Britain without learning anything definite.

One of Lucan's oldest friends, Dominick Elwes, the playboy artist, committed suicide in September 1975, at the age of forty-three. He had apparently been talking of suicide to his friends since June when he was blacklisted from various clubs at which he had been a regular visitor. He blamed the Lucan affair for having been used to stir up antagonism towards him:

If only 'Lucky' knew what he had let his old friends in for . . . He's damn near destroyed me [Elwes informed the *Daily Telegraph*]. If only he would come forward and give himself up. I know he's alive – he has got a lot to answer for. We were almost like brothers. Every day during our fifteen years of friendship we have always been in daily touch. I am sure he is alive somewhere and hiding in the most desperate circumstances.

The view expressed in the last sentence was not, as we have seen, one that was shared by all his friends. But the quest for Lucan continued and in November 1975, when a requiem mass for Sandra Rivett was held at Westminster Cathedral, four detectives including Ranson and Gerring mingled with mourners, presumably just in case Lucan might be present, if only in disguise. After the service Ranson commented that 'we are still actively pursuing Lord Lucan's whereabouts'. Since then there have been alleged sightings of Lucan in the Channel Islands, in Colombia and other parts of South America, and in Zimbabwe and Mozambique. A report came from a convicted murderer in an Italian prison (conveyed via a source in St John's Wood, London) that he had met Lucan some time previously in South America. The story gleaned by this convict was that Lucan was receiving funds regularly from a British resident in Barbados. That was in January 1978, but though Scotland Yard asked the Barbados police to investigate, there was no trace of such a benefactor.

By far the most interesting report on Lucan, however, came from Dr Brian Sandford Hill who claimed that he had spent two days with the Earl in Mozambique in April 1975. Dr Hill, who had been travelling from Swaziland to Mozambique, met an Englishman who was using the name of James. The latter was in the company of a Portuguese woman known only as Maria and, together with Dr Hill, they had dinner at the Perperri Restaurant in Lourenço Marques. During the evening Dr Hill happened to mention that he was shortly returning to Britain and the man James said he wished he could do so.

'Well, why can't you?' asked Hill.

'I am wanted by the police,' was the reply. 'I am Lord Lucan.'

Dr Hill, who had been out of Britain for some time, had not heard of the Lucan affair, so the man calling himself James had to explain the situation to him. 'The man who claimed to be Lucan was casually dressed and he seemed to have lightened his hair in some way,' said Dr Hill. 'He said he was heading for Kenya or Rhodesia, whichever country offered him the better prospects.'

The last Dr Hill saw of the man calling himself James was when he disappeared in a black Mercedes.

The police took this narrative seriously, not only because it seemed extremely factual and the description of 'James' tallied exactly with that of Lucan, but because Hill indicated no ulterior motive for volunteering such information to the police. They were unable to substantiate his story mainly because it was almost impossible to get any assistance from the Mozambique authorities. But one or two of Lucan's friends and some detectives think it is quite possible that, when he escaped, Lucan made straight for Lisbon. From there he might quite easily have reached Mozambique either by sea or air, providing he had forged identity papers.

The history of disappearing people reveals that again and again people develop strange quirks for posing as those who have vanished. After the disappearance in 1920 of the British MP, Victor Grayson, who was never found, over the years various people claimed in conversation with others: 'I was Victor Grayson, but am now living under another name'. So it may well be that Dr Hill and others have been the victims of some kind of hoax. Yet there is a great difference: Grayson disappeared for no apparent reason and was not wanted by the police; Lucan is wanted for murder, and to pretend to be a wanted murderer is a dangerous and unlikely hoax.

A bets 'book' on whether or not Lucan will emerge again is kept by one or two of his former friends. The odds vary from year to year and they are far higher against his being found now than in the year of his disappearance. The truth is that few can imagine just how Lucan would survive in such circumstances. 'I cannot imagine him as a mercenary soldier, as some have suggested,' said one friend. 'It is just feasible solely because he once was a soldier. But I can't see his keeping it up. I can't imagine 'Lucky' roughing it anywhere for any length of time.'

But when Detective Chief Inspector Gerring retired from the Metropolitan Police at the end of 1979, he expressed the opinion that Lucan was still alive and 'most probably in South America'. 'I believe he could have got away with the help of a friend,' he added. 'He could even have laid low in this country for a time while the hunt was at its hottest.'

4
'Hijack to Mogadishu'

'The fight in Mogadishu against international terrorism set an example of solidarity, an example which we hope will lead to joint endeavours of all people of good will, so that we can put an end to terrorism.'

STATE SECRETARY BOELLING
OF WEST GERMANY

It was approaching two o'clock on the afternoon of 13 October 1977, when the eighty-four passengers settled down in the Lufthansa Boeing 737, named Landshut, ready to take off from Palma, Majorca, for Frankfurt. They were mainly holiday-makers returning to Germany.

There was a crew of five, including the pilot, Jurgen Schumann, and the co-pilot, Jurgen Vietor, who had been called up an hour or so before the plane was due to leave. Passengers and crew were relaxed and waiting for the word to take off. There was only one really tense person aboard the aircraft and that was Hans Hasse Heyn, whose wartime experience as a Wehrmacht counter-intelligence officer possibly made him ultra-cautious. Before joining the plane he recalled the increasing frequency of aircraft hijacks all over the world. He had taken the precaution of having all his papers and documents photocopied so that there were duplicates left behind in Majorca of those he was taking with him to Frankfurt.

Security checks for passengers were minimal, even casual and jocular, possibly due to the fact that most of them were holiday-makers and that boarding the flight were some very attractive German girls who were finalists in a beauty contest for which they had been invited to Majorca. Two young men, who at other times and at other airports might have been subjected to special scrutiny, came aboard without any fuss. They were Youssef Akache, whose garishly coloured jacket did attract some notice, and Wabil Harb, a Lebanese who had fought on the Moslem side in his country's civil war. With them were a twenty-two-year-old girl, Suhaila Sayeh, born in Israel of Lebanese Christian parents who had emigrated to Kuwait, and Hind Alameh, another Lebanese Christian who had sympathised with the Palestinian Arabs' cause. If someone had thoroughly inspected their luggage, they would have been astonished to find, carefully hidden inside a large radio set, a make-up case and a false-bottomed suitcase, several pounds of plastic explosives, two East European pistols, ammunition and home-made hand grenades. All that happened was that the Spanish security guards had superficially looked into the make-up case, opened some of the quartet's hand luggage and gone through the usual motions of lightly frisking the clothes for concealed weapons.

The passengers were told to put out their cigarettes and fasten their safety-belts while the Lufthansa stewardess Gabrielle Dillmann walked down the tourist class cabin to make sure they obeyed instructions. The plane took off with Vietor at the controls. Almost immediately lunch was served. Half an hour later the plane was approaching Marseilles and the stewardess went into the galley to fetch a trolley to collect the passengers' lunch trays. She had noticed that Wabil Harb and Hind Alameh were in the first class cabin, while Akache and Suhaila Sayeh were sitting together in the tourist class. Suddenly she looked up in surprise as someone brushed brusquely against her, heading towards the cockpit. It was Youssef Akache.

Before she could do anything Akache, closely followed by Wabil Harb, entered the flight deck and they pulled revolvers from their pockets, weapons which they must have taken from their hand luggage as both men had been frisked before boarding the plane.

'Don't move! Turn round and keep your hands on the controls,' shouted Akache at the surprise pilots. He seemed excited, while Harb was quieter and much cooler. It was quickly apparent that the hijackers – for it was now obvious what they were – wanted Vietor out of the control seat and preferred to have the chief pilot in his place. Harb and Akache punched Vietor and pushed him away, urging him to 'get out of the cockpit'. He was hustled into the first class cabin with Harb's gun in his back.

This unexpected development created panic among the passengers and it was a full two minutes before calm was restored. Even then this was only achieved when Akache strode through the cabins, pistol in hand, telling everyone to raise their hands.

He was backed up by Suhaila Sayeh and Hind Alameh who dominated the gangway by menacingly revealing their hand grenades and shouting at the passengers to remain still if they valued their lives. Children started to cry and some of the older women sobbed. Vietor, knowing that the first rule when a hijacking occurs is to do as one is told, quietly urged the passengers to comply with the demands. He had himself been literally kicked and punched out of the cockpit. When an old woman collapsed in the gangway, Gabrielle Dillmann lowered her hands and bent down to attend to her.

'Keep your hands up!' screamed the Palestinian girl, Suhaila. Gabrielle complied.

Then Akache picked up the microphone and shouted hoarsely into it. His words came out in an incomprehensible jumble and nobody could make out what he was saying. He appealed silently to the stewardess as much as to say 'What shall I do?'

'You must speak much more slowly and carefully,' replied Gabrielle.

At last Akache made himself heard. He announced quietly and deliberately: 'This is Captain Martyr Mahmud. Keep your hands up, or you will be killed. Now pull down the blinds and throw all your knives and weapons into the gangway. Do as I say at once.'

Akache was a man with a split personality. One moment he could be rational, controlled and even cheerful, the next he was suspicious, irascible and excitable, almost paranoiac. Some passengers compiled with his request. For the benefit of most of the passengers Gabrielle Dillmann, at Akache's behest, translated his instructions given in English into German.

Meanwhile Akache gave the pilot Schumann his instructions: 'You are to go to Cyprus. Get out your chart and work out a route'.

Vietor was called in to get out the charts. After he and Schumann had studied them, the latter told Akache that Cyprus was outside the plane's range as they had insufficient fuel.

'For how long will it last?' angrily inquired Akache.

'Only as far as Rome, I should say.'

'Very well. We shall go to Rome and refuel there.'

It was at 14.38 hours that the air traffic controller at Aix-en-Provence reported a deviation from its route by the Lufthansa Boeing 737. This was the first hint that something unusual had happened. This report was carefully examined and analysed by State Secretary Ruhnau of the Federal Transportation Ministry. He decided that hijacking was a possibility and informed the Federal Interior Minister Maihofer. As a precaution the Minister immediately set in motion measures that had been pre-planned in case of a hijacking.

By the time the plane touched down at Rome's Fiumicino airport at 15.45 hours, the West German Government was already prepared for the worst. Then came a message to Maihofer from Rome that one of the hijackers had been talking to the control tower by radio. He was fairly incoherent and the gist of his message was that the group he represented demanded the release of their comrades held in German prisons: 'We are fighting against the world's imperialist organisations,' he added.

The Lufthansa company asked the Federal Government to act on their behalf. There really was no other alternative. Although no group had been named, Maihofer was fairly sure that this was a spokesman for either the Baader-Meinhof terrorist movement or the Siegfried Hausner Commando of the Red Army Faction who had recently kidnapped Hanns Martin Schleyer, president of the Federation of German Employers. On 5 September the Federal Government had had messages from the Red Army Faction Group who claimed to hold Schleyer and demanded the release of ten other terrorists from West German prisons.

The top security Stammheim Prison in West Germany

Ulrike Meinhof in Cologne Prison 1974

Andreas Baader in Paris

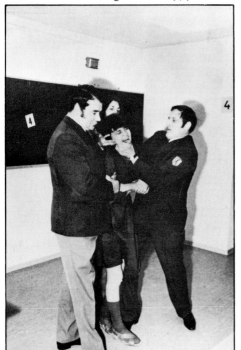

Jan-Carl Raspe

Irmgard Moeller

Gudrun Ensslin after her arrest in Hamburg, 6 days after that of her lover Andreas Baader

ESCAPE!

Herr Schleyer had been given a police escort because of earlier threats to his life by the Baader-Meinhof group, but his Mercedes and the escorting police car had been ambushed. Three guards and a driver were killed and Schleyer had disappeared. Nothing more had been heard of the industrial magnate since a tape recording made by his captors had shown that he was still alive and apparently unharmed, but showing signs of strain and fatigue.

'What has to happen to make Bonn make up its mind?' asked Herr Schleyer in this recording. 'I have been now in terrorist hands for five and a half weeks and I am here because I worked for years for this country and for its free and democratic system. Sometimes it strikes me what a mockery all this activity has been.'

Andreas Baader and three other leading terrorists, Jan-Carl Raspe, Ingrid Schubert and Gudrun Ensslin, were already serving life sentences in the top security wing of Stammheim Prison. Their future seemed to depend on the outcome of the Schleyer kidnap, but the West German Government was not prepared to exchange any of the prisoners. Hijacking was so much on the increase that it was felt to be imperative for governments to take a strong line against this type of blackmail. Earlier on there had been some humiliating capitulations to terrorist demands in various parts of the world and, encouraged by these surrenders and receiving of ransom money and release of prisoners obtained by such tactics, hijacking had become a profitable sideline for various underground groups.

The day before the hijacking of the Lufthansa plane Gudrun Ensslin had a message conveyed from prison that she wished to speak to State Secretary Schueler, head of the Office of the Federal Chancellor of West Germany. This request was considered by the SSMG (Small Situation Management Group), a committee set up to watch and advise on kidnappings such as that of Herr Schleyer, or hijacking. It was this committee which had decided to stand firm with the kidnappers.

On the morning of the thirteenth an official of the Federal Criminal Police went to see Gudrun Ensslin. When his visit was announced to her, she said she would not talk to a policeman, but only to a politician. She was informed that the State Secretary did not refuse to talk with her, but that such a talk would only have any meaning if the prisoner made known in advance the subject of the talk. She replied that this was merely an attempt to divide the prisoners from the kidnappers and to play them off against each other.

Then came news which positively linked the hijackers with the kidnappers, for at 17.00 hours on 13 October a message from the air traffic controller at Milan stated that a 'Captain Mohammed' had demanded the release of all 'comrades' imprisoned in West Germany. The Federal Interior Minister Maihofer thereupon contacted his opposite number in Italy. He asked the Italians to shoot out the tyres of the plane so that it could not take off.

However, the psychologist consulted by the Small Situation Management Group (a rather long-winded title for a body from which instant action was required) spoke out strongly against this suggestion. He argued that any such move could result in the whole situation getting hopelessly out of hand. The psychological effect on the hijackers was unpredictable. But they might become trigger-happy and start using their weapons. There was a real risk that they would threaten to kill the passengers unless they were given a free passage.

The psychologist was all for doing nothing for the time being, but to wait for a favourable moment at which to talk. At Rome airport the plane was guarded by troops, but no attempt was made either to attack it, or to enter it. The situation remained tense but quiet and at 17.45 hours the Lufthansa 737 took off for Cyprus after having been permitted to refuel.

Next came a telephone call from Stammheim Prison that Gudrun Ensslin wished to talk with a certain official. The prisoner was allowed to pass her own message over the telephone. She said she was prepared to talk either with the State Secretary, or his deputy, but not with any policemen. This time it was suggested that any conversation might be best conducted directly with Andreas Baader.

Meanwhile the Lufthansa plane's pilot had managed to indicate by radio that four hijackers – two men and two women – had taken control of the aircraft. This at least gave the SSMG a better chance of assessing the situation and weighing the risks. The chief difficulty was that they had no means of knowing exactly who the hijackers were or their psychological characteristics. But the Group discussed the situation at some length and it was agreed to initiate a pursuit of the Boeing 737. By arrangement with the Federal Government another Lufthansa plane, a Boeing 707, was ordered to take off from Frankfurt. Officials of the Federal Interior Ministry and Federal Criminal Police boarded the aircraft and, when the plane touched down at Bonn, members of the Border Police Group 9 joined them. Wischnewski, the deputy in the Chancellor's office, and the consultant psychologist, Wolfgang Salewski, were among the party.

Earlier experience had shown that in tackling hijacking problems, a psychologist was not only able to give valuable advice on the state of mind of the hijackers, but he could help to avoid provocative moves which might lead to mass slaughter. Governments all over the world had accepted that while a trained psychologist could not himself supply all the answers, he was an almost indispensable guarantee against total disaster. The order to the Boeing 707 was to intercept the hijacked plane at Larnaca in Cyprus.

The counter-action to try to save the lives of the passengers without giving in to the terrorists' demands had begun.

Meanwhile in the hijacked Lufthansa 737 there had been relative quiet, punctuated only by isolated incidents involving a few of the passengers.

After the hijackers had insisted on those aboard the plane throwing any pen-knives or 'weapons' down on the gangway, the passengers had been thoroughly searched. Not unnaturally, knowing that the hijackers were supporters of Palestine Liberation movements (even though they might be linked to and controlled by West German terrorist groups), the Jews among the passengers were the most afraid. They feared they would be singled out and treated roughly, if not killed. With few exceptions, however, such fears were groundless.

Hans Heyn, who had had a premonition of trouble before he set off, was hit across the face and poked by the barrel of a pistol when his searchers discovered that he had retained a nail file. They insisted that this constituted a weapon.

Akache was the most intimidating of the hijackers, often screaming at passengers on the slightest pretext. Suhaila Sayeh was equally harsh, if only in the manner in which she barked out orders, or made threatening gestures with her hand grenades.

Both the pilots had had some coaching in the psychology of handling hijackers; in this respect the West Germans had certainly shown foresight in giving their pilots talks on the subject. Their instructions were to keep as calm as possible, to do everything to ensure the passengers did what the hijackers requested and that they kept any conversation with their captors on rational terms without being too friendly. As they approached Cyprus there were talks between the hijackers and the two pilots. Akache asked Schumann to fix a microphone ready for him to speak. He told Schumann that he understood about flying, as he had trained on light aircraft in Britain.

There had been an incident just before this which struck the two pilots as slightly amusing, even if they felt in no mood to laugh about it. The plane had been radioed by another passing Lufthansa plane, going in the opposite direction. Seizing the microphone, the arrogant Akache had informed its pilot: 'This is Captain Martyr Mahmud from the Halimeh Commando, fighting against the imperialist organisations of the world.'

Obviously puzzled and oblivious of the drama that was being enacted aboard the Boeing 737, the pilot replied: 'I do not understand you. Please repeat,' and then broke contact.

This reply, thought the pilots, must have been rather a let-down for Akache.

They landed safely at Cyprus at 20.28 hours and received instructions from the control tower to turn around and taxi to the furthest end of the runway.

Federal Minister Maihofer had already been in touch with the Cypriot Acting Minister of Foreign Affairs, Andreas Patsalides. They agreed that it would be helpful to play for time and the Larnaca airport authorities made the excuse that there would be some delay in refuelling because the oil tanker's crew had gone to Nicosia and would have to be recalled. The hijackers had asked for eleven tons of fuel.

Then a representative of the Palestine Liberation Organisation – the PLO – came to the airport and entered into negotiation with Akache over the loudspeaker. He made an appeal first in English and then in Arabic, urging the hijackers to let the passengers go. The object of this exercise was to enable the hijackers to go free on the understanding they released their hostages. But this only enraged Akache who threatened that if there was any further delay in being refuelled, he would blow up the plane.

More talks between Maihofer and Patsalides followed, after which the Boeing 737 was refuelled and set off for Beirut at about 11.00 hours. Despite this delay, the pursuing Lufthansa plane did not arrive in Cyprus until after the hijacked plane had left.

Telephone wires had been buzzing all over the world since the hijacking and Bonn had kept in communication with London and Paris as well as all airports where it was thought possible the Lufthansa 737 might head for. The West German Chancellor, Helmut Schmidt, had been in touch personally with Britain's Prime Minister, James Callaghan, and France's President, Giscard d'Estaing. Both had promised to lend what support they could. At the same time arrangements had been made that the airports of Damascus, Amman, Baghdad and Kuwait should be closed to prevent the hijacked plane from landing.

In the early hours of the morning a message from Geneva positively identified the kidnappers of Herr Schleyer with the hijackers of the plane. The vital part of the message amounted to a demand from the terrorists:

Ultimatum to the Chancellor of the Federal Republic of Germany: we herewith notify you that the passengers and crew of the Lufthansa 737 aircraft, Flight Number LH 181, from Palma, Majorca, to Frankfurt/Main, are fully under our control. The lives of the passengers and the crew and the life of Dr Hanns Martin Schleyer depend on your meeting the following demands:

1. Release of the following comrades from West German prisons: Andreas Baader, Gudrun Ensslin, Jan-Carle Raspe, Verena Becker, Werner Hoppe, Karl Heinz Dellwo, Hanna Krabbe, Bernard Roessner, Ingrid Schubert, Irmgard Moeller and Guenter Sonnenberg.

Each person to be given 100,000 Deutchmarks.

2. Release from the prison in Istanbul of the following Palestinian comrades of the Popular Front for the Liberation of Palestine: Mahdi and Hussein.

3. Payment of 15 million US dollars, according to the attached instructions.

4. Arrange with one of the following countries for the admission of our comrades after they are released: Democratic Republic of Vietnam, Republic of Somalia, Democratic People's Republic of Yemen.

5. The German prisoners shall be brought to their target place in an aircraft made available by you. They shall fly via Istanbul and pick up the two Palestinian comrades released from the prison there. The Turkish Government is well informed

of our demands. All prisoners will reach their destination by Sunday, 16 October, 1977, 0800 hours GMT. The money is to be handed over within the same period of time, according to attached instructions.

6. If all prisoners are not released and fail to reach their destination, and in case the money is not handed over (according to instructions) within the above-mentioned period, Hanns Martin Schleyer and all passengers, as well as the crew of the Lufthansa 737 aircraft, Flight LH 181, will be killed at once.

7. If you comply with our instructions, all will be released.

8. We shall not establish contact any more with you. This is our last contact with you. You will be held responsible for any error and or mistake made in releasing the above-named prisoners and, or in handing over the above-mentioned ransom according to instructions.

9. Any attempt at delay and or deception on your part means the immediate expiration of the ultimatum and the execution of Hanns Martin Schleyer, the passengers and of the crew of the aircraft.

13 October, 1977,
Organisation for the Battle Against World
Imperialism.

Passwords were provided for the transmission of the messages so that the West German Government should be in no doubt that there was a link between kidnappers and hijackers. There was a second message which stated that Helmut Schmidt, the Chancellor, had now been given time enough to arrive at his decision.

He must choose between the American strategy of destroying liberation movements in Western Europe and the Third World and the Federal Government's interest in avoiding sacrificing the currently most important economic tycoon on the altar of imperialist strategy. The ultimatum of the *Kaffre Gadum* Operation of the Commando Martyr Halimah and the ultimatum of the Red Army Faction Commando Siegfried Hausner are identical. The ultimatum expires on Sunday, 16 October, 1977, at 0800 hours GMT. Unless the eleven prisoners have reached their destination by that time, Hanns Martin Schleyer will be shot dead. After forty days of Schleyer's detention there will be no further extension of the ultimatum. Likewise, no more contacts. Any delay means the death of Schleyer. To avoid a time lag, it is not necessary for Pastor Niemoller and Lawyer Payot to accompany the prisoners. We will get confirmation of the prisoners' arrival without the help of escorts. After we have received confirmation, Schleyer will be released within forty-eight hours.

Freedom by armed anti-imperialistic combat,
Commando Siegfried Hausner,
Red Army Faction.

Instructions for the delivery of the ransom stated that the 15,000,000 US dollars should be broken down as follows: 7 million in bills of 100 US dollars; 7 million DM in bills of 1,000 DM; 7 million DM in bills of 1,000

Swiss francs; 14.5 million DM in bills of 100 Dutch guilders. The ransom was to be carried in three black Samsonite suitcases, of three different sizes, with the combination lock set at 000. These suitcases were to be carried by Eberhard Schleyer, son of the kidnapped industrialist, who was instructed to wear a 'beige suit, with sunglasses in the breast pocket of the jacket. The frame of the glasses should be clearly visible against the pocket from outside. He should carry the latest edition of *Der Spiegel* in his left hand.' The instructions added that at some point during his trip he would be contacted by the Red Army Faction's representative who would say to him: 'Let us save your father'. He should answer: 'We shall save my father.'

The terrorists stressed that no attempt should be made to shadow Herr Schleyer junior, or to delay or impede him in the completion of his mission. He should arrive at the Frankfurt Intercontinental Hotel on Saturday 15 October, at noon local time, with the ransom money and his passport. There he should await precise instructions.

The terrorists had chosen a neutral country for relaying their messages, thus indicating how vulnerable even a country which tries to be neutral in all matters can be when it gets involved with international terrorist organisations. The intermediary chosen by them was a Geneva lawyer named Denis Payot, a member of a distinguished Swiss family, who had been president of the Swiss Human Rights League. He had shown an interest in various cases involving human rights and had shown some partisanship for the Arab cause. It was perhaps for this reason that he was singled out in the first place by representatives of the Baader-Meinhof group. Perhaps, too, someone of the name of Payot was chosen for psychological reasons, as in World War II one Marc Payot had been chief cryptographer of Swiss counter-intelligence. At any rate it was to this Geneva office that the final largely propagandist message to the West Germans was addressed: 'To all revolutionaries in the world! To all free Arabs! To all Palestinian masses!' It was a lengthy diatribe, telling how the Lufthansa 737 had been put under the command of 'our Martyr Halimeh Commando Unit' and that the aim was the liberation of their comrades from

the prisons of the imperialistic, reactionary Zionist alliance. . . . The expansionist and racist character of the Zionists headed by Menachim Begin is a product of imperialistic interests. . . . For the same reasons West Germany was built up as a US base in 1945. . . . The clear example of the close co-operation between the Mossad [Israeli Secret Service] and the German Intelligence Service, together with the CIA [US Central Intelligence Agency] and DST [French counter-intelligence] with the dirtiest policy of the imperialistic-reactionary alliance.

It continued in much the same vein, trying to compare Zionists with the Nazis.

By this time it was clear that the forces the West German Government was up against were an international conglomerate of anti-Zionists, Palestinian

Top left: Wabil Ibrahim Harb Top right: Youssef Akache Below left: Hind Alameh Below right: Suhaila Sayeh

The four terrorists who hijacked the plane: Top left: Youssef Akache and Hind Alameh Top right: Wabil Ibrahim Harb Below: Suhaila Sayeh. It is believed that these pictures were taken in Mallorca shortly before the hijacking

terrorists, Marxist and anarchist elements and the largely German Baader-Meinhof group. M. Denis Payot continued to act as intermediary between the West German authorities and the Commando Siegfried Hausner, but issued a statement that he accepted this mandate 'for solely humanitarian reasons', urgently requesting all parties involved 'to do everything possible to prevent a massacre'.

All this was a very obvious attempt to isolate the West Germans and to attempt to win sympathy elsewhere for their cause by attacking the Bonn Government. Helmut Schmidt was by reason of West Germany's membership of the Common Market an internationally-minded figure and therefore able to counter this ploy. The SSMG was in no doubt that he needed to assure himself of support from outside Germany before he committed himself too irrevocably to a policy of calling the hijackers' bluff. So one of his first moves was to win backing for his 'stand firm' decision from Britain's Callaghan and France's Giscard d'Estaing. Giscard said 'yes' at once; Callaghan, more cautious and with an eye on his Labour Party's divided views on the Middle East crisis, asked for an hour for discussions. But eventually he gave Schmidt his backing. This in effect meant Anglo-French approval for any counter-measures Schmidt might take in refusing the terrorists' demands.

Callaghan, though slow off the mark, actually proved even more helpful than Giscard d'Estaing, within a short time letting it be known that he not only backed West Germany, but was prepared to provide personnel in support of counter-action. He indicated privately that the British Government would loan to the Germans professional operators from the Special Air Service, the highly-skilled regiment formed during World War II for undertaking sabotage behind enemy lines, which in recent years had been used as an anti-terror squad in the Far East and Northern Ireland. For the Special Air Service, or SAS, as this unit is known, had already acquired considerable know-how, albeit some of it only theoretical, on new tactics for coping with hijackers. The British had taken the view that if hijacking was to be halted it was essential for it to be achieved on the basis of international co-operation, as only that would be regarded as a serious deterrent.

By this time there was no doubt about the determination, leadership and skill of the terrorists' controllers. Ulrike Meinhof, the daughter of an art historian, had studied philosophy and sociology in Germany, and together with Andreas Baader had given her name to the Baader-Meinhof group. This gang had always been associated with the extreme Left, but did not go underground until 1970 when Baader, who had been arrested on various charges, including arson, was rescued from prison. In the next seven years the group concentrated on building up cells, establishing contacts with other terrorist factions, creating its own 'safe houses', securing funds and indulging in such enterprises as intercepting police radio messages and organising a supply of weapons and explosives. By robbery and blackmail the group had built up funds of nearly two million marks.

Links were set up with Palestinian guerrillas, the Basque terrorist organisation, ETA (*Euzkadi ta Askatzuna*), the Black September gang and the Italian *Brigate Rosse* (Red Brigades), and out of this developed the Red Army Group or Factions. For the first time women were playing an increasingly important role in the sphere of terrorism. There were no fewer than twelve women among twenty-two activists of the Red Army Factions. A special feature of their way of life was a marked liking for champagne and vodka, gambling and high living in between their various operations.

Thus the Red Army Factions had been built up in the past decade into an extremely influential international terrorist movement able to switch its attention from Europe to the Middle East, from Germany to Spain or Italy, and with a network of hide-outs all over the world. It was for this reason that the SSMG referred its findings to the Chancellor's office which, in turn, had consulted with the British and French and, unofficially, with some Arab states.

A radio message informed the pilot of the 737 that Beirut airport was closed and he passed this on to Akache.

'Then try Damascus,' said Akache impatiently.

'They won't let us in at Damascus,' replied Schumann, who was now at the controls. 'They've blocked the runway.'

Akache became angrier and angrier as Schumann reported airport after airport closed. Baghdad was also blocked. Vietor suggested they might try Kuwait, as they had just about enough petrol for that trip. But Kuwait also refused to allow them to land and they were forced to head for Bahrain. Maihofer's pleas to other governments had borne some fruit. At last there were some signs of international co-operation against the terrorists.

At this stage instructions were given to the Lufthansa 707 pursuing the Landshut to take the commando team back to Cologne, while State Minister Wischnewski and his party were to be flown on to Ankara to wait there. At 01.52 hours on 14 October, the hijacked Boeing landed at Bahrain after having been told that the runway was blocked. In despair Schumann pleaded with the controller that they hadn't got the fuel to go on anywhere else.

It was a tense situation for Schumann because an agitated Akache was insisting he should land regardless: 'I don't mind how you do it, or where you land, but land you must.'

Luckily the controller appeared to be British and, though he again insisted that 'the officials here won't let you land', he passed on to him the automatic code.

'What's the automatic code?' Akache asked suspiciously.

'It's the code for an automatic landing.'

The route of the hijacked plane

A hijacker holds a gun aboard the plane

Jurgen Schumann the pilot (L) with his co-pilot Jurgen Vietor

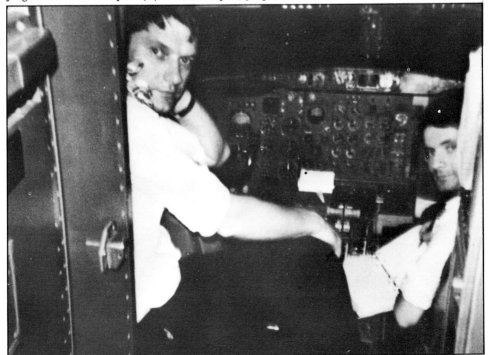

'Then go in,' urged Akache.

The plane landed in Bahrain in darkness and within seconds it was surrounded by troops. Akache picked up the microphone in one hand and waved his revolver around with the other: 'This is Captain Martyr Mahmud,' he told the control tower. 'If your soldiers have not gone in five minutes, I shall shoot the pilot.'

As though to emphasise his point, he turned to Vietor, who was at the controls, and said: 'You'll be dead in five minutes if they haven't gone by then.'

Schumann remonstrated that this was an unreasonable suggestion: 'You can't expect them to pull out in five minutes. These troops are not in direct contact with the tower.'

Vietor begged Akache to let him speak to the Control Tower. At length Akache relented and handed him the microphone. The co-pilot then firmly but briefly told Control that if the troops were not withdrawn immediately, he would be shot. 'A pistol is pointed at my head right now,' he added, to lend point to his plea.

After several anxious minutes the soldiers began slowly to withdraw and Akache gave instructions that they should refuel and proceed to Dubai. 'And from now on,' he added, 'you will call me Captain.'

It was at 03.24 hours on 14 October that the Lufthansa once again took off for Dubai. By this time the morale of the passengers was beginning to wilt. They had been mildly optimistic until the landing at Bahrain. Now they felt that, like the Flying Dutchman of legend, they were doomed to keep voyaging around the world without ever being given the chance to escape from the plane.

The flight to that point had been a testing time for crew, passengers and hijackers. All were beginning to reveal their virtues and their weaknesses. Many of the passengers would have succumbed to their fears and phobias if it had not been for the unremitting care of some of the crew and, in fairness, the solicitation of at least one of the hijackers. Gabrielle Dillman, the air hostess, won the friendship of shy and frightened children, but sometimes found it harder to cope with the old and confused. One passenger tried hard to reduce the tension by drawing sketches of some passengers and hijackers and showing them around. He took care to show them to the hijackers first. One such sketch drew a smile from Akache after one of his severe outbursts of temper which alarmed all of them. Yet occasionally he, too, could quieten down and crack a joke. Suhaila Sayeh was generally disliked by the passengers, as she was always shouting or waving her hand grenades in front of them. But with her it was really a case of the woman trying to show she was as tough as the men.

Schumann and Vietor were, of course, under perpetual strain. The moment anything seemed to be going wrong, Akache vented his temper on them and made threats. On the other hand Akache could on occasions make surprisingly humane gestures. Once he went down on his haunches in the gangway to talk to a small boy, not only offering him an orange, but actually peeling it for him.

There was about this time a certain easing of restrictions on passengers. They were at last permitted to talk to one another without being threatened. But the terrorists insisted on the blinds being down: they did not want the passengers to know exactly where they were. Nevertheless the shrewder among the latter were able to find out by listening closely to scraps of conversation. Water was drastically rationed out of sheer necessity. Except for one or two seriously ill cases, all that was permitted was a single sip. For several hours the passengers were not allowed to leave their seats and they just had to relieve themselves by wetting their clothes. Then, in strict rotation, they were allowed to go to the lavatory.

The hijacked plane approached Dubai and requested permission to land. Back came the reply that the runway had been blocked. For the next few minutes the plane circled round the airport at a height of 8,000 feet. Schumann repeated his request to land. Impatiently, Akache seized the microphone and poured out a torrent of words in Arabic.

While circling the airport, Schumann was able to note the lay-out of the place and in the early dawn to spot one narrow strip of concrete where a forced landing was just possible. He indicated as much to Akache. 'Take her down right away,' ordered the hijackers' leader.

So at six o'clock in the morning the plane touched down at Dubai, Schumann having radioed the control tower that they had to land, but giving no reasons for doing so against control's instructions. It was Vietor who brought the plane to a halt without any mishap, despite the fact that Akache's pistol was rammed into his back as he made the descent. Then Akache again took up the microphone and launched into his now familiar diatribe that this was 'the leader of the Martyr Halimeh Commando speaking', that if the ground forces at the airport did not follow out his orders, the plane would be blown up. He then made a request for refreshments.

Sheik Mohammed bin Rachid, Defence Minister of the United Arab Emirates, drove to the airport control tower to negotiate with the hijackers. Though it was already fiercely hot out on the tarmac, the kidnappers refused to release the women and children. Food was sent out to the plane and there was an easing up of restrictions on using the toilets. A special appeal was made for the release of one sick passenger, but Akache rejected all such pleas. His one concession was to allow a large spoonful of water to each person. The hijackers changed into what they called their 'uniforms', consisting of Che Guevara T-shirts. They were beginning to feel the strain and to suffer from lack of sleep.

Intermittently, Akache was on the look-out for anyone who might be

Jewish among the passengers. He not only scrutinised their faces, but would make periodical searches of their hand luggage in the hope of finding some incriminating evidence. On one occasion he whipped a fountain-pen from a woman's handbag, examined it closely and then went back to the bag and took out her passport.

'Birgit Rohll?' he inquired menacingly of the passenger.

She nodded nervously.

'You are Jewish', he shouted.

She denied this vigorously, but both Akache and Alameh kept repeating 'Jew! Jew! Jew!' They both pointed to the Star of Israel on her pen, insisting that it was a Jewish emblem.

In vain did the hostess Gabrielle Dillman try to point out to Akache that this was simply a trade symbol and that Rohll was a West German citizen. He slapped the passenger's face and hurled more abuse at her, hinting that she would be summarily executed as 'an enemy of the Arabs'.

The strain on the Jewish passengers was far worse than for any of the others. They could never be sure that Akache's hatred of Jews would not erupt into physical violence or an impromptu shooting. One Jewish woman managed to pass over to the air hostess a small item of jewellery which she surreptitiously wrapped in a piece of paper. She whispered that she was sure she would never be allowed to leave the aircraft alive, but, if Gabrielle Dillman survived, would she see that this treasured possession was given to her family.

One male passenger said afterwards that

I should have gone mad at one stage if I had not played noughts and crosses with myself. The chief of the hijackers thought I was writing messages in code and he hit me across the face and threw the paper he had snatched from me on the deck. Then he realised that he might be discarding vital evidence of a passenger's plot, so he bent down and picked it up. He went away and showed it to one of the girls. They looked back in my direction, suspicious and puzzled. I could not help smiling.

Eventually they cross-examined me about the noughts and crosses. What was the key to the code? Then I showed them the game and how it was played. It took a long time to convince them it was a game. But that little incident boosted my morale. I lost any sense of fear after that. Once they started to play noughts and crosses themselves – though it was only for half a minute – and began to laugh, I felt that a tense situation was relieved. From time to time Akache passed my seat, crossed two fingers and curved a thumb into an O, grinning at me and slapping my back.

A special meeting of the West German Cabinet was held on the Friday morning. Careful consideration was given to the commitments of the constitution to protect human life, to the results of previous hijackings and how to save the lives of the hostages. It was finally decided that, under Article 34 of the Penal Code, it would be neither permissible nor advisable to give in to the demands of the hijackers. What weighed most with the Ministers was the prejudicial impact a release of the prisoners would have on blackmail cases of all kinds and the danger that the release of even more prisoners would be demanded while the present kidnapping was still going on.

The Federal Chancellor then authorised State Minister Wischnewski to go to Dubai to discuss the situation with the authorities. Wischnewski then flew in from Ankara with Salewski and Commander Ulrich Wegener of the West German special force, GSG-9, to confer with Sheik Mohammed. In the meantime the hijackers had demanded penicillin for a sick passenger aboard the plane, but specifically declined medical aid. The Germans made no concessions and the hijackers stubbornly insisted that the plane would be blown up unless the prisoners were all released by the deadline given.

Then at six p.m. on the Friday the hijackers demanded eleven tons of fuel or a ground power unit to maintain essential services. The people at the control tower played for time and said they would pass the message on to the Minister of Defence. At intervals Akache talked to the two pilots. Schumann, a shrewd and cool operator, asked the terrorist leader if he really believed he could in all conscience kill so many people.

'Certainly,' replied Akache with assurance.

Schumann then asked whether Akache had actually cold-bloodedly killed anyone.

Akache responded by saying that when he was in London he had shot the Foreign Minister of Yemen, his wife and chauffeur. He had learned how to kill in a camp outside Baghdad. 'We Arabs', he added, 'have the same objectives as your urban guerrillas in Germany. We want to end the capitalist system and set the people free.'

Once, when he heard that it was the birthday of one of the air hostesses, a Norwegian girl known as Mia, Akache suddenly became convivial and in a party mood. He talked gaily about ordering the control tower to send them champagne and a birthday cake.

It was from small, isolated incidents such as this and from details contained in official dossiers on the hijackers that Wischnewski and Salewski gradually built up a composite picture of the kind of people they were dealing with. They knew that they were faced with two formidable and capable young girls, one rather quiet and less effective young man and a leader whose temperament was volatile and behaviour erratic. They also knew that all four were either Palestinian or Lebanese, but closely linked with the German terrorists and urban guerrillas.

Salewski was worried that Sheik Mohammed, not being well versed in the ways of terrorists, was employing the wrong tactics. He told Wischnewski that it was asking for trouble for Sheik Mohammed to refuse the hijackers fuel or ground power. 'You must play along with them and at the same time make them feel you can help them out of their dilemma,' he urged. 'You must keep up the dialogue with them. Talking is a safety-valve.'

The dead body of Hind Alameh

Youssef Akache

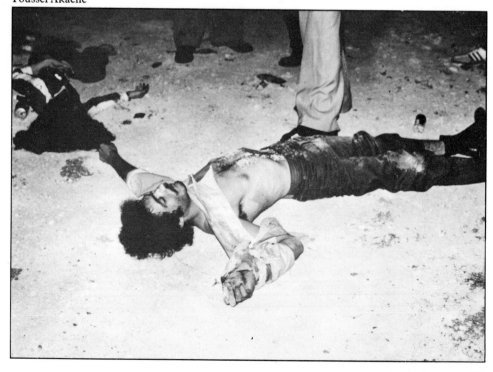

The hostages safely home

Gabrielle Dillman

Ulrich Wegener, head of the German Commando Unit

What both he and Wischnewski fully appreciated was that there must be no repetition of the disastrous attempt by the Germans to rescue nine Israeli hostages taken by Palestinians during the Munich Olympics of 1972. Since then the Germans had learnt a great deal and it was this specialised knowledge of coping with terrorists and hijackers that had enabled them to resist their demands. Ever since the holocaust at Munich a special West German commando unit had been in training for just such an eventuality as now faced them at Dubai. The whole purpose of this highly skilled unit was to tackle hijackers without putting their hostages at risk. The current situation was greatly complicated by the fact that it was taking longer than usual to build up an accurate psychological picture of the hijackers – a picture that would enable their reactions to be predicted if a rescue attempt was launched.

The key figure on which they had to concentrate, all agreed, was that of the unstable Akache. His parents had fled from Israel in 1948 and even as a teenager he had shown fanatical devotion to the cause of the Palestinians and joined George Habbash's Popular Front. Akache had come to London early in 1973 to study at the Chelsea College of Aeronautical and Automobile Engineering, living in a bedsitter in Earl's Court where he surprisingly kept tame mice as pets. The Germans had been given a dossier on him by the British, as Akache had been marked down by the Special Branch as a potential trouble-maker after he had attacked the police in a Trafalgar Square demo. But instead of deporting him forthwith, the British had allowed Akache to stay on in London as a student. Then in 1975 he had been involved in another fracas with the police and was sent to prison for six months. In this period he had gone on hunger strike. After that he was deported to Beirut in 1976, but returned to London the following year under the alias of Adel Hassan, a Kuwaiti. It was after this that he shot and killed the former Yemeni Prime Minister, his wife and chauffeur. After that assassination coup he vanished in the crowds and managed to slip out of the country undetected that same day.

Ulrich Wegener, the head of the German commando unit, tried in vain to persuade Sheik Mohammed to allow his men to be brought in. But the Sheik declined, saying that his own troops must deal with the situation. Both Wegener and Salewski were agreed that Emirate troops without any training in tackling hijackers could make things much worse. It was in the midst of such talks that news came through that Akache was demanding by radio some crates of champagne and a birthday cake.

On Salewski's advice these goods were delivered to the plane and this incident seems to have created a temporary relaxation of the tension in the Lufthansa 737. The birthday cake was decked out with twenty-eight candles and the crew and passengers mingled with the hijackers to toast the air hostess's birthday in champagne served in plastic beakers.

But this display of goodwill was not to last long. Akache decided after the toasting ceremony that he was going to give the passengers a lecture on the cause of the Palestinians and make a savage attack on Zionism. Telling them how he had been born in a refugee camp, he excitedly referred to the reason why the hijackers had called this operation Kaffre Gadum. 'A year ago the Jews attacked the village of Kaffre Gadum and killed everybody – men, women and children. That is why we want to destroy —— '

The sentence tailed off into nothingness. In his rising passion Akache had fired his revolver into the air. For a few moments there were screams and panic.

Perhaps Hind Alameh suddenly felt sorry for the passengers. At any rate after this pistol-shooting affair she alone among the hijackers began to show some remorse. When Akache was engaged elsewhere she patted a small boy on the head and gave him a small Spanish fan, smilingly saying 'It's to keep you cool'. To other passengers she gave reassurances that they would be quite safe and need not worry. Such gestures may have helped to alleviate the tension, but as one middle-aged man added: 'All the time it was like living in a cage with a tiger when Akache paced up and down'.

That night the power in the plane failed and still there was no sign of any fuel from Sheik Mohammed's ground force. To ease the stifling conditions inside the plane Akache gave permission for the cabin doors to be opened. It was not until the early hours of Saturday morning that a ground power unit was brought out to the Lufthansa 737. Even then an agitated Akache suspected this was a plot to gain access to the plane and he screamed that the men manning the trolley bearing the ground unit were spies. Schumann did his best to calm him down and explain that they must be given a chance to link up the unit to the plane. But Akache continued to argue that they were German soldiers wearing Lufthansa uniforms. He then accused Schumann of being in league with them and of having passed on secret information over the radio.

'You are a German Secret Service agent, aren't you?'

'No.'

'You were in the German forces, eh?'

'Yes, I was once a captain in the Air Force.'

Having obtained this admission from Schumann, Akache continued to question the pilot, threatening to shoot him if he did not tell the truth. Schumann admitted that he had informed those in the control tower that there were four hijackers and that they had pistols, grenades and explosives. Even after the power was restored, the lights came on and the ventilators started working again, Akache persisted in his tirade towards the pilot, accusing him of being a traitor. He made him march up and down the cabin.

For yet another torrid day the plane remained at Dubai. The temperature soared to more than a hundred degrees and the passengers' limbs swelled. Some of the women collapsed and had to be dragged out of the compartment and placed near an open door. This interlude placed a considerable strain on the hijackers who were more or less forced to relax their strict security regulations. 'I don't know why we don't try to escape,' said one woman, lying near the open door and slowly reviving. 'We could easily jump on to the tarmac. But I suppose they would shoot us if we tried.'

Some of the passengers actually moved into the first class cabin, which the hijackers had insisted was out of bounds. There they sat on packages of explosives and fuses. Maybe the hijackers were also suffering from the heat. Some of the female passengers were so oppressed by the high temperature in the plane that they stripped off everything except their knickers. Most of the men discarded jackets and shirts.

Food and drink were dispatched to the plane, but still there was no fuel. Schumann was permitted to send a telegram in his name to the German Chancellor. It stated: 'The lives of ninety-one men, women and children depend on your decision. You are our last and only hope. On behalf of the aircraft crew and passengers. Schumann.'

On the morning of the fifteenth the Large Political Advisory Group of the West German Government after a very long meeting decided that measures should be taken to free the hostages in the hijacked Lufthansa aircraft, if necessary by force. At the same time, following discussions with the SSMG, they informed Eberhard Schleyer by telephone that the ransom money could not be given to him because the place and date of the rendezvous had become publicly known. Monsieur Payot was also informed in his Geneva office that it was impossible to transport the ransom money in the proposed manner because of its weight. Meanwhile the Federal Criminal Police transmitted the following message for the kidnappers to Payot: 'Submit immediately proposals for the delivery of 15 million dollars under conditions which can be fulfilled.'

It was now rapidly becoming clear that few countries in the world were prepared to play along with the hijackers. Vietnam and South Yemen had refused to accept any terrorists. One country – Somalia – also named by the Commando Martyr Halimeh had not been mentioned by the prisoners in West Germany. So the Federal Criminal Police in Bonn checked through Payot whether Somalia would still be considered as a country for asylum.

The attempt to wear down the hijackers by playing for time, withholding fuel and other supplies, had obviously failed. Sheik Mohammed eventually gave in and the plane was refuelled. No hostages were released and no shots were fired at the Lufthansa 737. The hijackers had made two further threats to shoot the chief pilot and two passengers if the plane was not refuelled.

But in one respect the morale of the hijackers was punctured. On the Sunday morning of 17 October the ultimatum given by the kidnappers of Schleyer had expired. The Red Army Factions were not in contact with the hijackers so there was no question of joint discussions as to what their next move should be. At a quarter past twelve on that Sunday morning the hijackers said they would give sixty hours' grace for the fulfilment of the ultimatum and they demanded that the external power supply unit should be removed immediately so that the aircraft could take off. This concession was made and shortly afterwards the plane took off in the direction of Massira, heading for Aden. Here the South Yemeni authorities refused to give permission to land. From the plane the hijackers could see for themselves the presence of armoured cars on the runways.

Vietor, who was at the controls, indicated that he would crash-land in the sand. As he was shaping up to bring the plane down he noted that Akache had not fastened his safety-belt. Shouting at him to fasten up immediately, he pulled on the controls and tilted the plane up and sideways, a manoeuvre which brought a remonstrance from Schumann. Only when a somewhat abashed Akache had fastened his seat-belt did Vietor turn round to make his landing. This gesture by Vietor had probably prevented Akache from being hurled into the windscreen when the plane touched down.

Luckily the plane soft-landed without anyone being hurt, but the two pilots could not be sure whether any damage had been done. Schumann insisted that he should be allowed to leave the plane to examine the exterior. Reluctantly, the hijackers let him go and he took the opportunity to go to the control tower to try to negotiate for the release of the hostages.

Akache seemed to make up his mind that Schumann had deserted them. Anxiously and with growing anger, he paced up and down the cabin. Eventually he seized the microphone and blurted out the threat that 'if the German captain does not return instantly to his plane, I shall blow it up with everyone on board'.

As though to underwrite his threat he ordered the other hijackers to start wiring up the explosives. Suddenly, Schumann walked up the steps into the plane as though he were an automaton. He seemed exhausted and nerveless, as though he could no longer take anything seriously. There was something in his expression which made the passengers uneasy. Perhaps he had a premonition of what was to come.

Akache strode up to him, revolver in hand. He shouted in a mixture of English and Arabic, the gist of which was that Schumann had betrayed him. Very quietly and in a tired voice Schumann tried to explain that there had been 'difficulties'. Akache would not listen. He hit Schumann across the face and then shot him in the head. The pilot fell to the floor, blood streaming from his wound. It was quickly obvious that he was already dead. The hijackers left the corpse in the aircraft.

From that moment Akache assumed the role of captain of the plane, even to the extent of putting on Schumann's jacket over his T-shirt and also his peaked cap. Early the next morning the plane was refuelled and ordered to take off by the Aden authorities. Akache announced to the passengers that they were going to Mogadishu.

Hanns Martin Schleyer with his wife and family. His son is on the far right

The scene of the Schleyer kidnap; his chauffeur and three police guards were killed

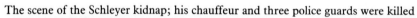

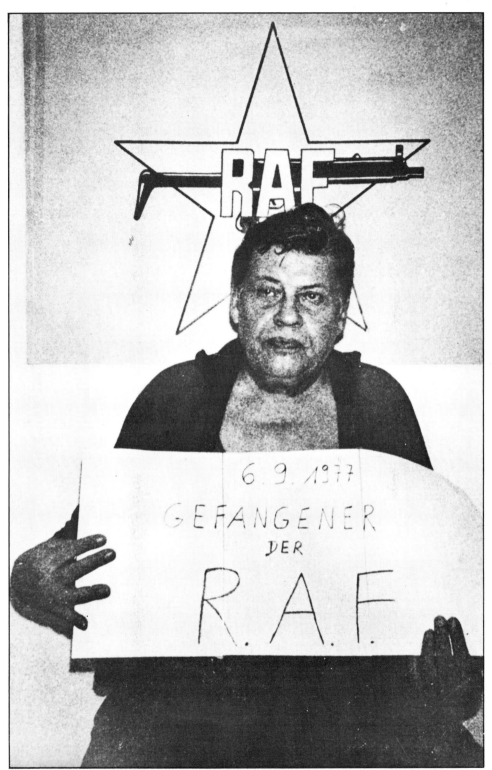

A photograph of Schleyer issued by the Red Army Faction

ESCAPE!

It was about this time that the West German authorities speeded up the emergency rescue plans. Ulrich Wegener, the tough and wiry chief of the GSG-9 team, had briefed his commandos. They had received a very thorough all-round training so that they could cope with all manner of situations from lock-picking to unarmed combat. He had had to leave his team in Ankara while he flew to Dubai to discuss the situation there. It was essential that his presence did not attract too much attention and he had some difficulty in disguising from Sheik Mohammed the fact that Germany had a contingency rescue plan. What Wegener needed to weigh up was what were the prospects for successfully storming the Lufthansa 737. The British Prime Minister had kept his promise to provide some expert advice in the persons of two Special Air Service men who used the under-cover names of a major and sergeant respectively. It was fortunate that Wegener already knew these men who were able to persuade him of the efficacy of a new weapon for tackling hijackers – a magnesium-filled grenade which exploded with such a brilliantly dazzling light and so loud a noise that an opponent could temporarily be put right off his guard and dazed for ten seconds, long enough for trained commandos to sprint sixty yards even when carrying equipment.

When Sheik Mohammed declined to allow the German troops to make any rescue attempt at Dubai, plans had to be changed rapidly. Since then it had gradually become apparent that the only real chance of success would be in Mogadishu if the hijackers headed there. This chance came when the Lufthansa 737 flew south round the Horn of Africa to Somalia and landed safely at Mogadishu airport in the early morning of 17 October. Schumann's body was unloaded down an escape-chute and the Somali authorities took it away in an ambulance. By this time a new commando team was on its way from Cologne to Mogadishu.

The Federal Chancellor asked the Somali Ambassador to come to see him. Later he talked on the telephone with President Barre of Somalia. The outcome was that the German Cabinet and the Government of Somalia agreed that a police action would be carried out to release the passengers in Mogadishu, either by Somalian forces alone or with German support, or by German forces alone.

Crew and passengers aboard the hijacked plane were now suffering acutely from the heat, lack of elementary hygienic requirements and especially the shortage of water. Those who were old and sick could not last out much longer. The stench was almost unendurable. Later that day Wischnewski, Wegener and Salewski arrived in Mogadishu with Rudeger von Lutzau as co-pilot and radio-operator. The last named had played a part in all the contingency planning. Together they all studied a large map of the lay-out of the airport which a Somali official provided for them. They set up their headquarters in a room behind the control tower.

Following negotiations with the hijackers over the radio, they managed to get the deadline for the ultimatum extended first by half an hour and later until 03.30 next day, thus allowing time for preparing the rescue. Back in the Stammheim Prison in Stuttgart an official from Chancellor Schmidt's office talked to Andreas Baader. The official reported back that

my task, in an exhaustive conversation with Baader, was to obtain as much concrete information as possible on what Baader wanted to tell State Secretary Schueler . . . I had the impression he was excited and nervous . . . he seemed to have a physical difficulty in articulating his words . . . The conversation revolved around the political aims and strategies of the Red Army Factions . . . He still regards the reason for their own activities – German support of the Americans in the Vietnam War – as an imperative reason for their operations . . . If they – the prisoners – had been released at an earlier date, they would certainly have been able to prevent the present brutal developments. . . . After their release they would, of course, stick to their promise not to undertake any further terrorist activities.

It was at 19.30 hours on 17 October that a special Lufthansa aircraft with a commando group from the Federal Border Police Group (GSG-9) landed at Mogadishu after dark, unknown to the hijackers. During the day some food and other refreshments had been sent out to the hijacked plane. Gabrielle Dillmann had taken over the duties of microphone spokesman with Akache's agreement. She made a desperate appeal for help, saying that they had people who were ill – 'one woman has cancer, one man is a diabetic. We can't go on another day in these conditions. You must help, or we shall be blown up. Why does the German Government hesitate?'

The game of bluff and counter-bluff went on. The hijackers ordered the women passengers to hand over all their tights and stockings so that, in the words of Harb, 'they can be used to tie you all up before we blow up the plane'. It was only by pretending to the hijackers that the prisoners in the German jails would all be released and flown to Mogadishu that Salewski, that wily psychologist, had bluffed Akache into agreeing to extend the deadline for blowing up the plane.

There were some sand dunes fairly close to the runway at Mogadishu, and under cover of darkness, it was possible to get within forty yards of the plane without being seen. This was an initial advantage; the psychological advantage was that the commandos were fit and eager for action, while the hijackers were becoming increasingly edgy, weary from lack of sleep and suffering from conditions in the plane.

The plan was for the control tower to occupy the attention of the hijackers by keeping them talking and, at the same time, to light a fire on the runway so that Akache and his three comrades would go up into the cockpit to see what was happening. While this was going on, the commandos would rush the plane from the rear. The commandos had had their final briefing from Ulrich Wegener and were kitted out with sub-machine guns, revolvers and grenades. While they were blackening their faces, preparatory to crawling

A pistol and a transistor radio found hidden in one of the cells used by the Baader-Meinhof prisoners in Stammheim Prison

The mother of Andreas Baader (centre) at the funeral of Baader, Raspe and Ensslin (see also below)

up to the sand dunes, Akache was looking at his watch and counting the minutes to the deadline. Recalling how the co-pilot, Vietor, had probably saved his life by insisting he strapped up his seat belt, Akache made a surprising gesture. He told Vietor he was free to go. But the co-pilot indicated that he was prepared to stay with the rest.

At midnight the GSG-9 commandos were in position behind the sand dunes. Two minutes later a diversionary bonfire was lit by Somali troops on the runway some distance directly in front of the Lufthansa 737. This was the signal for the commandos to move forward. Some of them carried ladders. Meanwhile the control tower tried to keep up communication with Akache.

The commando operation had been code-named Operation Magic Fire. It started precisely at five minutes past midnight. Before the hijackers had realised what was happening and while they were peering at the fire on the runway, two commandos opened the emergency exit window. Then the rear door was opened to let the others in.

'Down on the deck!' shouted the German soldiers. 'Everybody down on the deck. Get under the seats.'

Vietor had the presence of mind to dive under a seat just as Harb turned round and started to open fire. There was a confused burst of firing mingled with the explosion of grenades for about a minute, and a great deal of shouting. Harb was shot down almost immediately after he opened fire. Suhaila had the presence of mind to hide in the toilet. Hind Alameh was killed at the entrance to the cockpit. Akache was gunned down as he left the cockpit.

It was all over. Wegener ordered the passengers to leave the aircraft speedily in case it blew up. From the control tower at precisely seven minutes from the beginning of the operation State Minister Wischnewski was able to phone Chancellor Schmidt to give the code-word 'Springtime', which meant that the rescue had been carried out.

The only fear was whether there might be wired-up explosives which could blow up the plane. As the passengers were helped out they were told to get behind the sand dunes and lie low. It was an operation that went far more smoothly and at much less cost than anyone would have dared hope for a few days earlier. Only the air hostess, Gabrielle Dillmann, three passengers and one commando were slightly hurt. Suhaila was led from her hiding-place and put on to a stretcher, loudly proclaiming 'Long Live Free Palestine!'

This was one of the worst blows the terrorists, who had prided themselves on their international links, had suffered to date. The Terrorist International had been defeated by a shrewd, cautious and patient West German Government which had used its own international associations to bring about a rescue. Without the encouragement of other Western governments, West Germany's will to resist the terrorists' demands might have been weakened; without the backing of some at least of the Arab governments, the hijackers' morale would not have been undermined so quickly; without the help of Prime Minister James Callaghan, the invaluable magnesium-filled grenades and much sound advice would have been lacking; Sheik Mohammed in Dubai and the Somali Government had all played vital roles. German State Secretary Boelling expressed all this in a statement which said: 'The Government of Somalia, in deciding to allow us to undertake the operation, underwrote a precondition for preventing a catastrophe. The moral and political support which many other states gave us in our efforts to rescue the hostages and the crew from dangerous criminals was of great help to the Federal Republic of Germany.' In this same statement Boelling made an appeal to the kidnappers of Hanns Martin Schleyer to release their hostage.

At o8.58 that same day the German Press Agency reported that Andreas Baader and Gudrun Ensslin, who had been sentenced to life imprisonment, had committed suicide in Stammheim Prison that morning. Later it was announced that Jan-Carl Raspe had also killed himself, and that Irmgard Moeller had attempted suicide.

The passengers from the Lufthansa 737 were taken back to Frankfurt for what amounted to a heroes' welcome. They, too, had played their part by maintaining a quite remarkable degree of patience, stoicism and freedom from panic. But even more so had the crew of the plane helped to sustain their hopes and morale. As for the commandos, they had greatly enhanced their reputation as an efficient anti-terrorist squad, showing how such a rescue could be effected without loss of life to hostages, crew or soldiers. Minister of State Wischnewski paid his own tribute: 'The fight in Mogadishu against international terrorism set an example of solidarity, an example which we hope will lead to joint endeavours of all people of goodwill, so that we can put an end to such terrorism.'

But the rejoicing was swiftly cut short later that day when a rumour spread that Schleyer's body had been found in France. Then at 16.21 hours the Stuttgart office of the German Press Agency received a telephone call from a woman who gave this message:

After 43 days we have put an end to the deplorable and corrupt existence of Hanns Martin Schleyer. Mr Schmidt [Chancellor Schmidt], who – in his power calculations – has speculated on Schleyer's death from the very beginning, can now pick him up. He is in a green Audi 100 with Bad Homburg licence plates which is parked in the Rue Charles Peguy in Mulhouse. His death is meaningless in relation to our grief and rage about the massacres of Mogadishu and Stammheim. Neither we, nor Andreas, Gudrun, Jan, Irmgard, were surprised by the fascist drama of the imperialists aimed at the destruction of the Liberation Movement. We shall never forgive Schmidt, nor the imperialists supporting him, for the blood that was shed. The battle has just started. Freedom through an armed anti-imperialist battle.

The West German authorities immediately contacted the French to ascertain the truth of this report. Then occurred one of those farcical delays which have so often typified the processes of French criminal investigation. The French prosecutor and the Mulhouse magistrate each claimed the right to examine and identify the corpse, if one should be found. After lengthy arguments the Prosecutor won his point. He was, however, all for caution, suggesting that the message to the German News Agency could be a plot to lure unsuspecting officials into a booby-trap, and that there might be a bomb in the boot of the car.

A bomb disposal squad was requested, but there was a further delay in finding one. Some hours later, houses in the vicinity were cleared of all occupants while the car in the Rue Charles Peguy was located. Inside was a trunk which, when opened, was found to contain the body of the kidnapped President of the Employers' Union. There were three bullets in his head.

Schleyer's family were perhaps understandably bitter. While the hijacked hostages had all been rescued, he had been left to his fate. There was a feeling that the West German Government had regarded him as being dispensable. It was a natural, if unfair judgement. President Scheel was the only official to attend the funeral which the family wished to be kept as quiet as possible.

There had to be an investigation of the suicides in Stammheim Prison. Little time was lost by the underground supporters of the dead prisoners (and for that matter by Human Rights organisations in Western Europe) in suggesting that Baader, Ensslin and Raspe had been murdered by officials. Baader and Raspe had shot themselves, Irmgard Moeller had stabbed herself with a blunt prison knife, while Gudrun Ensslin had hanged herself. When found, Raspe was still alive and they took him to hospital at once. He died an hour later. Moeller was also alive and, after an operation, she actually recovered.

The West German Government was seriously concerned that the favourable international reaction to events at Mogadishu could be wiped out overnight by suggestions that the Baader-Meinhof prisoners had been murdered. After all, it was hard to explain how closely guarded prisoners could have got hold of pistols. In an effort to dispel such suspicions and counteract criticisms it was proposed that observers from other countries should be invited to be present at the post-mortems. Invitations were sent to Austrian, Belgian and Swiss professors. Lawyers for the Baader-Meinhof group attended the post-mortems, much to the indignation of the prison staff as it was their opinion, shared by the police, that only visiting lawyers could have smuggled guns into the prison and handed them to Baader and Raspe. These same lawyers now strongly represented to the world's press that suicide was impossible.

But the final verdict was suicide. And later a parliamentary inquiry revealed not only a certain amount of slackness in security at Stammheim

Prison, but cunning on the part of the prisoners in maintaining their own electronic communication system between their respective cells without its ever having been discovered and hiding places for weapons in both Baader's and Raspe's cells. The radio communications link had been ingeniously established by using an electric razor circuit.

The Baader-Meinhof gang and the Red Army Factions may have taken a severe beating by the authorities, but in the midst of the events of Mogadishu these organisations had shown an astonishing resilience and a talent for dominating and influencing public opinion even from beyond the grave. The very fact that they could get guns smuggled into prison suggested that they might well have infiltrated the prison security system. It still seems astonishing that lawyers would have risked smuggling arms into prison, yet if they were not guilty, who was?

And despite the deaths of the prisoners the Baader-Meinhof group has remained powerful, especially in its ever-extending links with other terrorist organisations, not least in connection with the ruthless kidnapping and murder of the Italian politician, Aldo Moro, in 1978.

5
'The Cartland Murder'

Frederic Delaude, a young man employed as a press officer with the Société Ricard in Marseilles, was motoring along a quiet country road in Provence shortly after midnight on Monday, 19 March 1973. He had left Montpellier late on Sunday night to drive back to his home at Aix-en-Provence.

There was a strong wind blowing that night and the trees were swaying like marionettes against the bright moonlight. As Delaude turned a corner he instinctively slowed down as he noticed what seemed like a fire about a hundred yards from the roadway on his right-hand side. There were flames and smoke, but exactly what was causing this Delaude could not tell as scrub and bushes obscured his vision. Then he saw that a caravan was burning and that someone was stepping out of the bushes on to the roadway waving his hands.

'I saw he was signalling me to stop,' Delaude told the French police the following day. 'I cannot tell you what time it was. I hadn't a watch on me. As soon as I stopped I opened my door and saw a man who was holding his stomach. He said to me, "I have been attacked." He also told me he had received two knife wounds.'

As Delaude left his car and drew closer to the stranger he saw that he was a slim young man with streaks of blood on his face and who clutched his stomach with one hand as though he was in pain. He had an English accent.

'What happened?' asked Delaude.

The young man pointed to his chest and stomach with the other hand and said that he had been with his father, but did not know what had happened to him.

Delaude walked towards the caravan which was now burning fiercely. The roof had fallen in and only the lower half of the walls was left. But, when he peered inside, there was no sign of any other person. At that moment another car approached from the direction of Aix-en-Provence so

Delaude stepped into the roadway and waved it down. Inside were a Madame Sobanski and her daughter. He told them briefly what had occurred and asked if they would notify the police and request them to get to the caravan as speedily as possible. They agreed and drove on.

Within a minute another car approached, this time a small white Renault, with three young men in it. They stopped to inquire about the fire. Together with Delaude they walked over to the caravan, shielding their faces from the fierce heat of the flames. One of them disconnected and removed the gas cylinder which was on the ground in front of the caravan, while another suggested they should move the car used for towing the caravan before it, too, caught fire.

The young man, obviously distressed by what had happened, seemed anxious to see a doctor. His name was Jeremy Cartland and he had been travelling across Spain to France with his father, camping out en route in the caravan. The three newcomers – Chambonnet, Lorenzo and Weltman – were eager to help in any way they could. They moved the car away from the fire as best they could, but the steering-wheel locked, so one of them asked Cartland for the car keys. Having secured them, they moved the car further away from the fire before trying to put out the flames. These had spread from the caravan to the grass and here they had to stamp out the fire with their shoes. Finding a drum half full of rubbish, they threw this into the caravan fire, subduing the flames to some extent, though the caravan itself was then a total wreck.

It was at this stage that Delaude, realising that Jeremy Cartland was in need of medical assistance, suggested he should sit down in his car. Later, as Cartland seemed to be in pain, Delaude agreed to drive him to hospital at Salon-de-Provence. Just as they had left the area, they were passed by a police patrol car.

The firemen and police arrived on the scene within an hour, after the fire had been completely extinguished. They immediately conducted a search for clues and the missing Englishman. Sergeant Manson took preliminary statements from the three young men who had stopped to fight the blaze. Then, while searching some bushes opposite the burnt-out caravan, they found the body of John Cartland, hidden in the undergrowth, his head almost severed and his body still warm.

Chief Warrant Officer Labourdenne directed a more intensive search for clues and a request was made for police reinforcements. There was, however, no really systematic search for forensic evidence. Next morning in daylight one gendarme drew a sketch of the area and the actual scene of the crime, while another took photographs. It seemed as though some attempt had been made to hide the body. The man was lying on his stomach, his feet pointing in the direction of the caravan, his legs stretched out, but his right arm was folded in a square under the body. He was wearing brown moccasin-type shoes with high tops, green socks and a pair of pyjama trousers were round his ankles, while the upper part of his body was dressed by a vest with two pullovers over this.

The autopsy carried out by the French authorities revealed that the face was covered with blood and pine needles and there was evidence of blows which had inflicted a severe caving-in of the skull.

The police managed to turn up some fairly obvious clues in the vicinity of the caravan site. There were a bloodstained kitchen knife and axe of a type often used by campers, and they came across a cushion-cover and some wrapping-paper in the undergrowth, both of which articles contained traces of blood. The police felt confident that one, if not both of these weapons, had been used for an attack on John Cartland. Clearly this was a case of murder.

In the hospital of Salon-en-Provence young Jeremy Cartland was carefully examined by the duty medical officer. He had a wound high up on the right side of his chest and another on the left side of his abdomen. Neither appeared to be very serious and the doctor, Dr Jean Louvard, expressed the opinion that after a couple of stitches in each all should be well.

Cartland had various bumps and scratches and the doctor, much to his surprise, extracted blood from his arm. 'I was later to wonder, as I became more aware of the circumstances of the case, just where that blood might have been sprinkled!' he somewhat sardonically commented later.

It was probably because they did not know what kind of a weapon had inflicted the wounds on young Cartland that the X-ray examination was prolonged. Afterwards even Cartland stated that they 'took what seemed an inordinately large number of exposures . . . compared with being X-rayed in an English hospital, this seemed a long drawn-out process'.

Jeremy Cartland frequently inquired during that night and the next day whether there was any news of his father, but mostly he received evasive answers. Once the director of the hospital told him 'Yes, your father is here, but in another part of the hospital.'

Dr Louvard asked Cartland how long he thought he had been unconscious. Jeremy replied that he did not know but thought it must have been at least ten minutes. 'When I came to, I was some distance away and the caravan was well alight.'

Sometime later Christian Gandon, an officer of the Judiciary Police, called to interview Jeremy Cartland in the hospital. He then told his story fully. The painstaking officer wanted to know all about Cartland's background and that of his father, and, of course, all details he could remember of the events of the previous day up to the time of the attack in the early hours of the morning. It is perhaps useful to look at the official report of what he told this officer at three o'clock in the morning of 19 March 1973.

Having told how he and his father had 'crossed the frontier at Col du Perthus', he briefly described their journey until they stopped for the night at a place which was known locally as Jasses-des-Dames, though Jeremy

Cartland did not himself know its name at that time. He told M. Gandon:

It was at about seven p.m. . . . When we stopped, with my father I unhitched the caravan to turn it round so as to be ready to leave next morning. We did not hitch it up to the car which we left two metres away from our caravan. We ate inside, then I did some accounts and we went to bed. It must have been about ten o'clock. Before going to bed I lit our paraffin heater.

When I had gone to sleep I heard voices outside. I got dressed to see what was going on, but before that I woke my father so that he could come with me. Before he was completely dressed I went out of the caravan and saw a person in our car, on the left-hand seat. I went towards him to see what he was doing. When I arrived level with the back of my car I called to the man who was inside, leaning forward slightly as if he wanted to touch something under the dashboard. I think at present that he perhaps wanted to connect the wires to steal our car.

I only saw the man from the back because right after I called I received a blow behind my head and lost consciousness. I do not know for how long I was unconscious, but when I came round I saw that our caravan was on fire. I went towards the caravan, the door of which was open, but I did not see my father inside.

I went to the road to stop a passing motorist. He was alone in his 2CV and was coming from the direction of Salon.

From that point onwards Cartland's evidence bore out all that was later described by the car driver who took him to hospital and the later witnesses of the fire.

Clearly, the French police had asked the doctors and nurses at the hospital to say nothing to Cartland about his father's body having been found. Meanwhile the police and the judiciary authorities were moving with speed in their inquiries. They had interviewed all the people whose cars had stopped at Jasse-des-Dames, including the mother and daughter, and some inquiries had been made in nearby villages. On the morning of 19 March M. André Delmas, examining magistrate, and M. de Bonfils, clerk of the court, were shown the scene of the crime by Warrant Officer Yves Salendre. The investigation of a crime committed in France is conducted under the supervision of an examining magistrate, the *Juge d'Instruction*. He directs the activities of the police and they report their findings directly to him. Ultimately he is the man who decides whether or not to prefer charges.

This was the first major criminal case which M. Delmas had handled. It also proved to be his last. He went to the caravan site at eleven thirty on the morning of 19 March, together with Warrant Officer Salendre, and Commissioner Krikorian of Marseilles. After inspecting the whole area in the vicinity of the burnt-out caravan he gave orders to the police doctor and her assistant to examine Jeremy Cartland at the Salon hospital as well as to carry out an autopsy on the murder victim.

Later that day Jeremy was visited by John Edmonds, the British Vice-Consul in Marseilles, and Frank Benham, the Pro-Consul. They, too, had

John Basil Cartland as a young man (centre)

John Basil Cartland (left) with a family friend, Conrad Miller-Brown

French police at the site of the burnt-out caravan

Jeremy Cartland revisits the scene

been told by the French authorities to give Cartland no definite information about his father. Jeremy persisted in asking about his father's whereabouts and eventually he was told: 'He has been beaten about the head like you. He is in a very bad way and is still unconscious.'

A tortuous game was already being played with the young Englishman. It was a civilised game, there was no harsh treatment, no undue pressure, no intimidation, but it was nevertheless a relentless, patient, probing test of his reactions. What struck Cartland as being curious was the final remark by the visitors from the British Consulate: 'We've been in touch with your family. Somebody will be coming from home tomorrow.' What did they mean? Why should they want somebody in his family to come over, especially as he expected to be up and out of hospital within a short while? And who was this 'somebody'?

Then there was a further examination of him by the police doctor, Jacqueline Jouglard. She made a laboriously detailed examination of his whole body, measuring 'every scratch and bump' was how Jeremy Cartland put it.

He began to be even more worried when later he was given an electro-encephalograph test. This test (usually known as an EEG) makes a record of electrical events in the brain. Nerve cells generate small electric currents that can be picked up from the surface of the scalp and shown on a cathode-ray tube. By using several leads from different parts of the scalp the electric patterns from different regions of the brain can be studied. These tests are still very much in the experimental stage, but they have been invaluable in confirming the diagnosis of epilepsy and some other disorders of the brain. All Cartland was told was that the police surgeon was testing for brain damage, an answer which was misleading to say the least.

Then came a lengthy interview with Commissioner of Police Gregoire Krikorian, a detective who had already won for himself a formidable reputation in the South of France. With him were a detective named Ettori, who took down Cartland's statement as dictated by Krikorian, a woman who acted as interpreter and another policeman named Gal. Cartland protested that he was tired and felt that the information he had already given to the police was enough. But Krikorian persisted, not merely going over the ground covered by the previous questions put to the young Englishman, but probing into the relationship between him and his father.

That same day Cartland's sister, Elizabeth, and a family friend, Ian Smith, arrived in France and were met by the two officials from the British Consulate. On the way to the hospital one of the consular officials suggested stopping for coffee. 'I thought this was rather strange at the time,' said Elizabeth Cartland afterwards. It was during this halt for refreshments that the consular officials broke the news that, though Jeremy's condition was satisfactory, the French police had not yet informed him that his father was dead. This in itself was a shock, but what followed was even worse. Gravely, but tactfully, they indicated that the French official view was that the murder was the result of a family quarrel.

The consular officials wanted to know how father and son got along together. Elizabeth insisted that they 'got along very well indeed'. She added that they worked very closely together as they had a common interest in the language school at Brighton which Cartland senior had founded. This interest was even extended to the vacations when father and son often holidayed together while seeking pupils in France, Switzerland, Germany and Italy. In reply to other questions as to whether her father's death might have anything to do with his wartime service, Elizabeth could not help very much with this line of inquiry.

All this questioning made Elizabeth's friend feel somewhat uneasy and resentful. He, like Elizabeth, was appalled when they were informed that the police had not told Jeremy that his father was dead. When they arrived at the hospital a police official told Elizabeth that she could not see her brother until Commissioner Krikorian had finished interviewing him. While she was waiting, another police officer, Chief Inspector Roustan, came to question her in a somewhat aggressive manner. He insisted: 'Your father and Jeremy must have had a quarrel.' Spiritedly, she replied that she could not accept this. She added that her father lived only for his children and that Jeremy loved him. Her brother had given up his own home and gone to live in Brighton to be near his father. He was 'a very gentle man and never quarrels with anyone'.

Later that evening Elizabeth Cartland was allowed to see her brother for a short time. Even then she was only allowed to stay for a few minutes and the brusque Commissioner Krikorian, together with the consular official, Frank Benham, and a typist were present all the time. Jeremy's own comment on their meeting was:

It was good to see a familiar face, and even better that it should be Liz. I was surprised to see her at all, because I really didn't think the situation was serious enough to warrant her coming all the way from England. She didn't say very much. She just told me not to worry and that she would soon take me home.

Elizabeth Cartland had not said very much because she had been told not to tell her brother what had happened. Only after she had gone did Frank Benham from the British Consulate tell Cartland his father was dead. He gave no details, but these were filled in later in a most devastating manner by Commissioner Krikorian. He drew a bloodstained knife out of a plastic bag and asked Cartland if he could identify it.

Jeremy replied that it looked like a kitchen knife, but that he had never seen it before. Krikorian insisted that they thought it came from the caravan. He alleged it was a type of knife not made in France – but later investigations proved that it had in fact been made in France. The bloodstains on it were, he alleged, of Jeremy's own blood group, and in

Krikorian's opinion it was the weapon that caused the young man's wounds.

Then, having waited for that item of information to sink in, Krikorian produced another package and took out of it an axe. Had Cartland seen that before? Yes, it had belonged to his father who had brought it with them on their trip. It was then that Krikorian opined that this was the axe with which Cartland senior had been killed.

There were a few more questions whereupon Krikorian demanded that it would be much better if Cartland told the whole truth quickly. Divisional Inspector Jean Ettori, who accompanied Krikorian, then tried shock tactics on the considerably harassed Cartland: 'We are of the opinion that you struck your father down with this axe.'

Accusations of a drunken brawl with his father followed. There were interminable questions about both the axe and the knife. Over and over again these questions were repeated, first in one form, then in another. It was only after ten o'clock that night that the detectives gave up their interrogation. Jeremy then felt that they were satisfied with what he had told them and that the interrogation was at an end. But as far as the French police were concerned the interrogation proper had only just begun.

John Basil Cartland was born in London in 1912. He was educated at Bradfield College and Worcester College, Oxford, where he obtained a double first in modern history. He left Oxford in 1933 and for a brief period took a teaching post at Cranleigh School. But Cartland when a young man (and for most of his life for that matter) was far too unconventional and adventurous to take up school teaching as a permanent career. He yearned for travel and excitement and very soon he found both when he went out to India. True, this was yet another teaching post at the Islamia College in Peshawar, but it enabled him to get out of a rut and to enjoy in uninhibited fashion life on the North-West Frontier. While he hunted, went shooting and played cricket, he also mixed with the Indians and learned something of their languages and customs.

From India Cartland went to the Sudan where he learned Arabic and later became education officer in the territory of the Blue and White Niles. When war broke out in 1939 he gradually moved into the sphere of intelligence work, eventually serving under General Wavell in Cairo. He must have impressed his senior officers, as within a short time he was sent to London to join the Political Warfare Executive where he was mainly concerned with propaganda. Then in 1943 he was transferred to the Italian section of Political Intelligence of the Foreign Office at Woburn Abbey.

Details of Cartland's wartime work are, however, difficult to come by and some of his own claims of what he did are not corroborated by independent evidence. During 1943 he married a young nurse named Joan

Wheeler and the following year his son was born and christened Jeremy Bryan Cartland.

Certainly Cartland claimed to be working for British Intelligence in Brussels at the end of 1944, saying that he had managed to find some dossiers about collaborators which the Gestapo had not had time to destroy before they left their building in the Avenue Bernard. According to his son, he burnt these files, believing that, with the war practically at an end, the 'business of revenge' was unnecessary. This sounds a remarkably unlikely story, as it was certainly not up to anyone in his position to make such a decision. But he appears to have told this tale to others besides his son.

Cartland senior made a brief entry into politics in the 1945 General Election when he stood as a Conservative candidate at West Willesden in London where he was soundly defeated. The next year he became assistant secretary of the Oxford University Appointments Board, which involved finding jobs for graduates. This post did not last for long and Cartland's next move was to Geneva where he worked for the United Nations Special Agency helping to resettle refugee graduates. All this time his marriage was under considerable strain, largely because Cartland was intolerant, argumentative and tempestuous in his relations with his wife. A daughter had been born in 1946 and, when the Geneva job ended, he became a partner in a preparatory school at Eastbourne. This did not last long as Cartland quarrelled with his partner.

Shortly after this his wife divorced him on the grounds of physical cruelty, and Cartland went off to Kuwait, again dropping hints that he was engaged in Secret Service work. It is now very difficult to judge when Cartland was telling the truth, as so many of his stories were embellished and some of them were flatly contradicted even by his friends. What is, however, undoubtedly true is that Cartland returned to Britain via Egypt, Libya and Tunisia and suddenly appeared to be quite affluent, sufficient at least to buy a house in Brighton and establish a language school. His son states that his father's story was that on his way back to Britain he had

dropped in to see his old pal Snusi [presumably he meant the Amir of Cyrenaica who became first King of Libya in 1951] . . . It was a grand reunion with much talk of the old days when they had fought together against the Italians. As he was leaving, Snusi handed him a suitcase and told him not to open it until he got home. He then caught a bus to Tunis so that he could take a ship back to Europe, and sitting there in that bus, amid a crowd of natives, he opened the suitcase and found that it was full of dollars.

The two Cartland children were in the custody of their mother after the divorce, though their father had access to them from time to time. Later both he and his ex-wife made second marriages, but in Cartland's case it was yet another disaster and lasted only a short time. There is ample evidence that father and son got along quite well and together they had made a

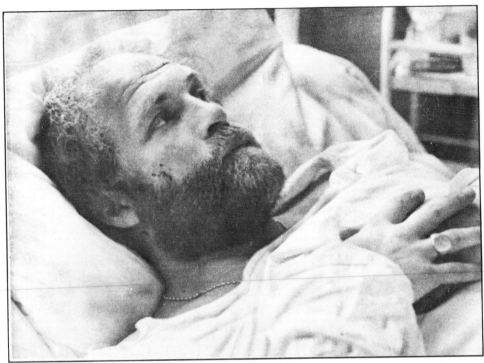

Jeremy Cartland in the hospital at Salon-de-Provence

Jeremy Cartland showing his wounds to his sister Elizabeth

Elizabeth Cartland

A Press Conference

number of trips to the Continent ever since Jeremy Cartland left school. It was on one of these trips, which were chiefly to the South of France, that Cartland senior met an American woman who was to be his second wife, Leila Nash-Hirschfeld, and, as seemed to be the custom with him, he proposed to her shortly afterwards. The old adage of 'marry in haste' seems to have been wasted on him. This time the marriage lasted five years until Leila left him and there was another divorce.

Both in London, where he was attending the College of St Mark and St John, and in Bristol, when later he had a teaching post, young Cartland often accommodated his father for the odd night or two in his flats. Finally, in 1972, it was agreed that Jeremy Cartland would join his father at Brighton and assist in the running of the language school, which concentrated on teaching English to foreigners. For some time Cartland senior had been fortunate in having the services as housekeeper and secretary of a Miss Janet Gibson, who later made a statement to the British police concerning him.

He was a quiet person, full of fun, moderate in all his habits, he was not a heavy drinker, smoker or spendthrift, though he wasn't mean with his money . . . There was never any suggestion at all that he might have been a homosexual, nor was he a womaniser . . . .

The relationship between Mr John Basil Cartland and his son Jeremy was friendly. I never knew them to have a quarrel . . . At the time they departed to the continent on 12 March 1973, John and Jeremy were very friendly as usual. The object of the trip was partly holiday and partly business and they wished to pick up their caravan at Denia, Alicante, from the land of Mr Lyon from whom they bought it.

Such is the rather scant picture one has of John Basil Cartland. It is true this is mainly a glimpse of the man as he was viewed by his family and house-keeper and, as far as his career was concerned, by his obituary in *The Times*. One of his oldest friends at Oxford, Sir Denis Wright, of the Diplomatic Service, wrote that John Cartland was 'brilliant and unconventional to the point of eccentricity'. Quite why someone who had scored a double first in history at Oxford and had considerable experience overseas undertaking important work should have failed to make anything of his life after the war remains a mystery.

In May 1971, John Cartland purchased a caravan in Spain, as described by Miss Gibson. His plan was to use it for touring Europe, while at the same time he hankered after buying a small property in Spain, or the South of France. The caravan was left in Spain until father and son went to pick it up in March 1973. It is significant that even at this stage in his life he was, according to Nicholas Lyon, from whom he bought the caravan, 'very talkative about his past and in particular his involvement in French Resistance activities during the war'. He was constantly telling people about these alleged activities, upon which no light is shed in *The History of SOE in*

France, which covers a very great deal of Resistance work and of British contacts with the various groups and networks. On the other hand the records of SOE (Special Operations Executive) activities in France during World War II had suffered considerably from wilful destruction and censorship before this history was written, and not all Resistance groups had links with SOE. Mr Lyon met both father and son and he 'heard no indication of ill feeling' between them. The only thing that struck him as odd was that Cartland senior should buy a caravan for £300 in 1971 and then wait two years before he collected it.

There were, however, various perfectly straightforward reasons for this as the Cartlands' plans had been upset for various reasons. En route to and from Spain they hoped to make contacts to provide some pupils for their school the following summer. They left Denia on 17 March, stopped at Gerona for a meal and spent the night in a motorway car park. When they awoke on the morning of the eighteenth the caravan had iced over and there was ice on the car which young Cartland chipped off. Cartland senior was in a hurry to get away from Spain and they did not stop for any length of time again until they reached Arles. There they visited the ruins of the Roman amphitheatre. At approximately seven o'clock that evening they reached Salon-de-Provence and stopped to buy petrol on the outskirts of a small town called Pelissane. Three kilometres beyond there they came to the clearing beside the road at Jasse-des-Dames and decided to settle down for the night.

Six hours later the caravan was burnt out and John Cartland was dead.

Since World War II there had been a number of cases of mysterious murders of British citizens while motoring across or camping in France, especially in the south. Many incidents involving rape, violent attacks and harassment had given the French tourist authorities a good deal to worry about. In certain areas of the country foreign visitors had received a very bad impression. The situation had become worse, if anything, after the entry into France of thousands of Algerians after the civil war of the late fifties. Some of these constituted a floating population of roving criminals. Yet the preliminary police investigation report contradicted this by asserting that there was not a large number of foreign workers in the area.

The killing of John Cartland aroused consternation among the French police as well as those interested in tourism because of its similarities with the notorious Dominici case which had caused such an uproar for several years. In 1952, while they were camping for the night at Lurs, a mere thirty-five miles from Jasse-des-Dames, Sir Jack Drummond, his wife and daughter had been murdered. Drummond, like Cartland, was said to have had associations with the French Resistance during World War II. The local population had been singularly unhelpful when the police investigated this crime, but eventually a farmer, Gaston Dominici, despite protestations of his innocence, was convicted. His death sentence was commuted to life imprisonment and in 1960 Dominici was pardoned and released by President Coty. There was a feeling that the wrong man had been convicted and this undoubtedly paved the way to the pardon.

One link between the two cases was that Cartland had known Drummond during the war and had on one occasion at least been with him in Brussels. Not unnaturally, given these facts and factors, an imaginative corps of journalists posed the question – was Cartland murdered by enemies he had made in France, either in the Resistance or among Nazi collaborators? It was not an unreasonable question considering that the same query had been made about the Drummond family.

But if the press liked to play on such melodramatic themes, the French police certainly veered away from any such suggestions which they regarded as either disconcerting mischief-making, or the prejudices of the xenophobic English. As one detective pointed out, an ex-Resistance man would have been more likely to use a gun than this barbarous method of killing. They were very anxious to play down this type of speculation because, once it was thought the Resistance and the British Secret Service might be involved, they could see the case being complicated by the involvement of the DST (the French Internal Security organisation) and the Special Branch of Scotland Yard and the respective Foreign Offices of the two nations.

Nevertheless the possibility of a revenge killing for some incidents dating back to the war years could not be ruled out. A year after the Drummond murders a German prisoner who had been in France confessed to a British Army Investigation Branch officer that he and three other men had been hired to kill the Drummonds. Nothing appeared to have been done to follow up this astonishing statement, but a former warrant officer in the British Army has made this statement to the author: 'The confession made to one of my officers preyed on my mind for years. I have often wondered what further inquiries were made.'

Though this is inconclusive evidence, it has some support even on the French side in an indirect way. In the same area – in Pelissane, to be exact – in the summer of 1944 a married couple named Cartier were killed in circumstances comparable to those of the Drummond case. The detective investigating this case was found shot dead in a ditch soon afterwards. When the Drummond murders occurred it was suggested that there was a link between that case and the Cartiers. But careful inquiries have revealed that there was no evidence to confirm this theory. The only positive link which the French detectives were able to establish was that Drummond knew the Cartiers during the war and had had several contacts with them. Nothing was found to associate the Cartiers with Cartland.

However, the French police relentlessly pursued what they felt was by far the simplest route to solving the problem, building up a dossier against Jeremy Cartland as the only other person known to have been in the vicinity of the caravan at the time of the attack on his father. Fate had played Jeremy the cruellest of tricks: from the police point of view he was the one suspect on whom to concentrate and he was not only in a foreign country, but in one where, unlike Britain, the suspect was deemed to be guilty until he proved himself innocent. Was it for this reason that the police did not appear to have looked for any other suspect, or carried out any thorough forensic examination around the site of the murder? There was the added advantage that he was not a Frenchman. If he could be proved guilty, there would be no bad publicity for tourism. Whereas if they failed to nail the crime on Cartland junior, the whole affair would probably remain an irritating mystery.

The French detectives first of all tried to show that Jeremy Cartland's own injuries were self-inflicted and that he caused these in an attempt to suggest that he, too, had been attacked and therefore was unable to defend his father. The detectives also argued that if assailants had killed the father, they would almost certainly have killed the son as well. And if Jeremy had been hit on the head and knocked unconscious, there should have been more medical evidence to support this. But there were, of course, strong arguments against such theorising. Firstly, few sane and well-balanced people would have inflicted such injuries on themselves even to cover up their own crime, and Jeremy was certainly perfectly sane. Not even under persistent cross-examination did he show any signs of being otherwise. There was no obvious motive for Jeremy to have killed his father. He had no expectations from his father's will and in any event had money of his own. But, for the French police, he was the only available suspect.

The detectives could not prove that the injuries to Jeremy were self-inflicted, they could only speculate that this might have been so. Their main line of inquiries concerned the murder weapons and the mystery of the locked door of the car. The official statement regarding this latter point was that 'no trace of breaking in was found on the left-hand front door of the car, which, according to Cartland, John Jeremy, was open since an individual seemed to be trying through this door to connect the wires. The door was found closed when the investigators arrived.' The police concluded that the murder weapon was the axe which was the Cartlands' own property and which Jeremy stated his father had insisted on bringing with them. Why should the prospective killers not have provided themselves with a weapon before setting out? One answer to this could have been that the murder was not premeditated and that two nocturnal prowlers just happened to come across the caravan, and that they had been disturbed while trying to steal something.

The question of the locked door of the car was one on which the police repeatedly questioned Jeremy. He had told the police that the car door had

Krikorian and Delmas confer

British Detectives on the scene: Detective Chief Superintendent Ronald Page, Detective Constable Claude Jeal, Sergeant John Troon, Sergeant Jo Gunn

Jeremy Cartland flanked by his sister and his mother on his way to
Heathrow

27 March 1973:
Jeremy celebrates with Liz at her wedding

been left unlocked since they left Arles, but that when he came out of the caravan on that fatal night, having heard noises, he saw 'a person in our car, on the left-hand seat . . . I think that perhaps he wanted to connect the wires to steal our car. I only saw the man from the back because right after I called I received a blow behind my head and lost consciousness.' The witness Chambonnet, however, while stating that the car doors were shut when he arrived on the scene, could not remember whether they were locked. Later he added that after the police arrived he went back to the car and 'saw clearly that three doors were locked'.

Jeremy Cartland's contention about these matters was upheld by a Madame Arlette Blasco who, with her husband, was motoring past the blazing caravan about three-quarters of an hour after midnight. M. Blasco stopped his car and got out to have a look. He saw two men moving around the caravan. Both he and Madame Blasco confirmed that later they saw one of the men leaning in through the front left-hand door of the car.

There was a shock for Jeremy when he had dressed to leave hospital. He was told by two plain clothes police officers that they were taking him to the police station to collect his possessions. When he reached the hospital doors he was greeted by a horde of newspapermen and photographers. The police had to force a way through the crowd for him to enter the waiting car. As soon as he got to the police station another interrogation began. There were questions as to what he and his father had drunk that night. Jeremy said he had had a glass of wine and a whisky and his father had just a glass of wine. They suggested that he and his father had a drunken fight and that scratches on Jeremy's face were made by his father, even though they had no forensic evidence to back this up.

How did he think the fire in the caravan had started? Jeremy replied that it was possible his father had knocked over the paraffin stove in his hurry to get to him. But was he in such a hurry that he wouldn't stop to pick it up? To this there was no obvious answer. The questioning went on until eleven o'clock that night when, according to Jeremy, even the detectives were beginning to yawn. At the very last they tried hard to get him to confess to the murder. Only at this late hour were the British consular officials able to negotiate Cartland's release into their charge. For two days he stayed with his sister in Marseilles. It was abundantly clear that the French police desperately wanted to bring a charge of murder against him and that he needed legal representation if he were to withstand all the pressures.

Nobody fought more strenuously on Cartland's behalf than his sister. It was largely through her efforts that the consular officials obtained his release from the police. Both John Edmonds and Frank Benham handled a difficult situation with skill and helped in finding lawyers to defend Cartland. One such was Christopher Mitchell-Heggs, a British lawyer practising in Paris. Until this point it had been touch and go as to whether French police tactics would succeed in view of Cartland's ignorance of complex

French legal procedures. They had taken full advantage of the fact that (again unlike British law) when a suspect is in hospital the demands of the police come first and the doctor's second. When he was at the police station they had neglected to tell him what his rights were: that, for example, he had the right of silence.

Mitchell-Heggs, together with Maître Paul Lombard, a distinguished French lawyer in Marseilles recommended by the Englishman, along with Maître Chiappe, who was head of the Bar Council in Marseilles, agreed to take up Cartland's case. They met at the house of John Edmonds, the Vice-Consul, and there advised that Jeremy and his sister should bring civil actions against 'a person or persons unknown' for the murder of their father. By doing this they could prevent Jeremy from being interviewed any further by the police. The effect of such action was that he could now only be interviewed by the examining magistrate and only then with his lawyers present.

This move to some extent eased what was becoming an extremely critical situation for Jeremy. Until this time he had been slowly exhausted both physically and mentally by the stress of prolonged interrogations in hospital and police station.

One of the blunders which one French detective had perpetrated was to make the truly astonishing suggestion to Elizabeth Cartland that, according to her brother, 'she and I had plotted father's killing before we left England'. This only had the effect of making Elizabeth determined to fight them all the way and defend her brother more vigorously than ever. Jeremy paid her a deserved tribute when he wrote afterwards that 'without her determination, her unquenchable spirit, her constant support and encouragement and above all her love, I believe I might not have survived the ordeal intact'.

From then on a cat-and-mouse game ensued between the French authorities and Cartland's legal advisers. The police applied for a warrant required for interviewing Jeremy on another matter altogether – arson relating to the caravan. But the Prosecutor-General rejected this application, presumably on the grounds that there was no more evidence to justify an arson charge than one of murder. To compensate for this failure the French police continued to regale the local journalists with their own account of the murder at Jasse-des-Dames. Even before this the detectives' off-the-record narratives were blazoned across the pages of the French press, implying as strongly as they could that Jeremy had killed his father. The young man did not have the protection of British libel laws.

Cartland agreed to attend a court hearing at Aix-en-Provence to appear before the *Juge d'Instruction* in five days' time. His advisers were strongly in favour of his returning to London first. They pointed out that, as he had not yet been charged with anything, he was free to go and the court could not withhold his passport from him. So Elizabeth and he flew back to England where he saw his mother and other members of his family. Jeremy took one important step on the occasion of this visit to London: he consulted an English doctor regarding the injuries which the French police had alleged were self-inflicted. He also took the precaution of having himself examined by Professor James Cameron, a Home Office pathologist.

Then on 27 March he returned to France with his sister, taking rooms in a hotel in Aix-en-Provence. The hearing, which was really an examination of Cartland and not a trial, took place on the following day in the chambers of André Delmas, the examining magistrate. The early questions put to Jeremy concerned the place they had chosen to stop for the night. M. Delmas wanted to know why they had chosen Jasse-des-Dames when there was an official camping site only a short distance further on. Jeremy replied that as they were strangers to the area they could not know there was a proper camping site nearby. Then he wanted to know why Jeremy had not discovered his father's body after he regained consciousness.

Cartland pointed to the fact that it took the police after their arrival on the scene, and several other witnesses of the caravan fire, at least half an hour before they found the body. Questions such as these did not take matters much further and, as the decision as to whether or not Jeremy could be charged lay with the examining magistrate, the police appeared to be irritated by his fruitless probing.

One point which Cartland's lawyers seized on were some gross inaccuracies contained in the official police sketch map of the scene of the crime. They also asked for a copy of all the medical reports made on Jeremy when he was in hospital as well as having a copy of the autopsy on John Cartland. These should have been made available under regulations to all parties concerned. In the meantime they had prevented the cremation of John Cartland and asked for a second autopsy by Professor Cameron, a British forensic expert of high repute. As a result of these tactics and of growing doubts by the examining magistrate about whether the police had any case to offer, there was a further adjournment and no charge was made. Nor, it would seem, did the police follow up any other line of inquiry.

Jeremy was requested to appear for a second hearing on 4 April and once again he went back to England, where he engaged a British lawyer as well to look after his interests.

It was at this time that an anonymous letter was received both by the *Daily Express* Paris Office and the BBC which expressed the view that there was a 'secret service connection' with the Cartland killing. The letter was typed in French and there was no signature. It was a somewhat rambling and confused missive of several hundred words and much of it was seemingly irrelevant. In the main it tried to link the Cartland murder with those of the Drummond family. 'Mr Jeremy Bryan Cartland's instituting a civil action allows one to suppose that a secret British council is also concerned in this affair, because of other facts noted by secret services,' suggested the writer somewhat obscurely. He went on to assert that the conviction of Gaston Dominici 'allowed one to think that the judiciary direction of that affair had not been conducted as it should have been. Rumours say that Sir Jack Drummond was the victim of important war secrets, some of which concern Indo-China.'

The anonymous scribe mentioned what he called 'the murder' of Sir Oliver Duncan in a clinic in Rome in 1964. The official view at the time was that he had fallen from his bed and broken his neck. Duncan had been an MI 6 operative at one time. He also referred to 'the mysterious death of Mr Michael Lasseter' in January 1973. Lasseter, a seventy-one-year-old former British Intelligence officer who had been living alone in Cannes since his wife died, was described in *The Times* obituary as 'a retired British Army officer'. The report added that he had died 'after being attacked outside his home'. It was thought that his death might have something to do with a manuscript he was sending to his publishers – a war diary. The manuscript was never found after his death.

The facts contained in this lengthy letter were all correct as far as they went, but the writer produced no positive evidence to link any of the cases he mentioned with that of John Cartland's murder. But it did have the effect of turning the attention of the media towards the possibility of a Secret Service involvement, an element of mystery to take this affair out of the realms of a mere commonplace killing. This in turn made both British and French authorities somewhat uneasy as to what else might be made public.

Eventually the anonymous scribe was traced to one of those compulsive writers to the newspapers on a wide range of subjects, though mainly those concerned with espionage. His name was Polydeskis. But there was nothing he could say which would point to the identity of a possible killer, or provide evidence which would assist Jeremy to establish his evidence.

So the investigation dragged on, with the police now more intent on finding a motive for the murder than searching for more clues. All manner of suggestions were made and duly ventilated in the French press, one of them being that father and son had quarrelled over a woman. Needless to say there was not the slightest evidence of any such thing. Nor was there a financial motive. The sole beneficiary of John Cartland's will was Miss Janet Gibson, his secretary-housekeeper. He had made ample provision for his two children during his lifetime. Despite all efforts by the French police to try to establish a bad relationship between father and son, certainly all their British friends testified to the contrary. Then again the French had tried to suggest there had been a drunken brawl late that night at the caravan and that both men had had too much to drink. The independent autopsy on John Cartland carried out by Professor Cameron of the Institute of Pathology of the London Hospital showed that 'alcohol was not detected in the urine sample; there was less than 10 mg alcohol per 100 ml in liver blood'.

What must have tested to the full Jeremy Cartland's powers of endurance was first, the growing realisation that nobody seemed to be looking for any other suspect, and, secondly, how the representatives of the media appeared to be merely waiting for charges to be brought against him. When he returned to France on 3 April for a further hearing of his case, it became obvious that the police were thrashing around for any tiny item that would provide them with a lead. This time the questioning centred on the possibility – already speculated upon in the French press – that there might be a woman in the case and that father and son had quarrelled on this account. No evidence was produced to support the allegation.

Once again the Cartlands – brother and sister – went back to England to await yet another hearing a few weeks later. It was during this session that Cartland received another nasty shock. The magistrate, André Delmas, informed Jeremy's lawyers that he had been given a message from Interpol stating that Professor Cameron had described Jeremy as 'a liar who could not be trusted'. If this had been true, of course, it would have been a serious and unexpected blow for the defence. But during the lunch adjournment of the hearing Mitchell-Heggs put in telephone calls to London to contact Professor Cameron. Eventually Mitchell-Heggs was able to produce a telegram from Professor Cameron which categorically denied that he had ever made any statement about Jeremy Cartland either to Interpol or anyone else. Jeremy's lawyer also applied for an annulment of the entire hearing on the grounds that the evidence was not shown to them twenty-four hours before the hearing in accordance with French law. They also warned that they would take out a suit charging the French police with attempting to falsify evidence and pervert the course of justice.

How the French authorities could have conjured up this particular allegation of a statement by Professor Cameron shows a singular ignorance on their part of the Hippocratic oath and a doctor's code of conduct. This may not apply so rigidly in France, but Jeremy's English counsel was sufficiently aware of its strict application in Britain to know that it was almost inconceivable that Professor Cameron could have made such a statement. His only worry was whether he could get a denial from the British pathologist in time to satisfy the French court.

This blunder may have paved the way to the halting of the hearing. The examining magistrate almost beamed down at Jeremy Cartland as he told him: 'You will be glad to hear that you will not be charged with killing your father.'

There was first of all intense relief both for Jeremy and his sister and then a brief celebratory dinner with the lawyers. But it was soon apparent to both of them that the French authorities had no intention of halting their case against Jeremy. In other words, the nightmare was to continue; the threat of arrest would remain with him. They heard that the French detectives were making inquiries in Spain about the purchase of the caravan. Commissioner Krikorian even went over to London to make inquiries, being assisted by Chief Superintendent Ronald Page of Scotland Yard.

Another hearing was set for 17 May, this time for that peculiarly French feature of criminal investigation – a reconstruction of events at the scene of the crime. Elizabeth Cartland flew out to Marseilles to find out exactly what was going on while her brother waited for a message from her that all was well and that he could safely come out. Cartland was quite prepared to return to France and to their courts, if by doing so he could help to clear his name, but his lawyers advised him that this would be inadvisable unless the examining magistrate could guarantee his freedom from arrest.

That guarantee was not forthcoming and in the end a message came through advising him not to travel to France. Later that day it was announced that the French police had issued an international arrest warrant for Jeremy Cartland. But this announcement proved to have been based on a bad translation of what the prosecutor really said, for there was no such thing as an 'international arrest warrant'. What, however, the French could do was to apply for Cartland's extradition.

So Jeremy had a few months longer in which to live with this nightmare. An extradition order was expected almost daily, but it never came. An attempt was made to try to enlist Home Office support for an inquiry into how the false statement attributed to Professor Cameron originated. The Home Secretary at that time was Mr Robert Carr and he merely replied that, as investigations were still in progress, 'it would be wrong for the Government of this country to become involved in any aspect of the case before the French legal processes have run their course. That is not to say that if in the end there appeared to be a denial or miscarriage of justice we should not take any steps open to us to remedy matters. We certainly would.'

There may have been more than one reason why the French did not apply for an extradition warrant. It is true that the political and secret service elements introduced, however irrelevantly, into the affair were not exactly helpful to Anglo-French relations and memories of the Drummond murders and the Dominici conviction and finally his pardoning lingered on. The French Minister of Justice, M. Jean Tattainger, consulted the President, then M. Pompidou, and the Prime Minister, M. Mesmer, and they eventually decided that there should be no request for extradition. Then on 11 July the French handed over the whole case, including their own evidence, to Scotland Yard.

This was, of course, a classic example of passing the buck. Just as Commissioner Krikorian had gone over to England to make inquiries about Cartland's background, so now did a British detective go over to the South of France to conduct his own investigation. Once again Jeremy had to relive in Britain the same agony he had endured in France. It was not until

18 December that he had a request from Chief Superintendent Page to attend Scotland Yard for an interview.

It was perhaps singularly ironic that, having taken all this time to conduct their investigations, Scotland Yard should suggest a date only four days before Christmas for an interview. Cartland was about to leave for Scotland where he was to spend the holiday at his mother's home. His journey had to be postponed. The interview at Scotland Yard was formal but polite. Jeremy himself said afterwards that 'there was no attempt to "put words into one's mouth" as there constantly was in France . . . When I was cautioned there was no doubt that I was still being considered a suspect.'

Then on 4 January 1974, the Metropolitan Police issued a statement which indicated that there was insufficient evidence for the institution of criminal proceedings against Jeremy Cartland. Not suprisingly, Cartland did not find this a satisfactory ending to the investigation, glad though he was that his ordeal was over. It was almost as though the powers-that-be were saying 'you are free to go, but . . .' But what? The case remained open. Were they merely grudgingly admitting that it was simply a matter of not being able to find sufficient evidence to bring a charge?

In this situation Jeremy Cartland fully realised that he had very narrowly escaped the guillotine in France, but that for once English justice had failed to exonerate him. In Scotland there is such a verdict as 'not proven'. In England the tradition is that if one is found not guilty, or if there is insufficient evidence to bring a charge, then one is innocent. Even the *Law Society Gazette* commented on the Metropolitan Police statement that

as the decision was apparently taken by the Director of Public Prosecutions, any public statement ought more properly to be issued by this office, not that of the Metropolitan Police. . . . Moreover the statement itself, by restricting itself to purely legal terminology – although intended for public consumption – leaves an area of doubt remaining by the use of the phrase 'evidence . . . not sufficient to warrant . . . criminal proceedings'. If any degree of doubt regarding Mr Cartland's innocence should now be unequivocally discounted – as is presumably the spirit of the statement – then surely this should have been expressed in language not capable of misconception by the layman.

A statment that said simply 'The DPP has decided that there are no grounds for instituting criminal proceedings against Jeremy Cartland in respect of his father's death' would have left no doubt in the public's mind as to the decision taken. In official statements from legal authorities exactitude in these matters is important because they are so capable of wide misconception.

One had the suspicion that the phrasing of this statement from the Metropolitan Police could have been influenced by someone high up who wished to save the face of the French police rather than to clear Jeremy Cartland. It is not entirely irrelevant that at this time the British Government had just entered the European Community and was courting France with an ardour unsurpassed for many years.

Jeremy had escaped from a frightening situation. Only a miracle would enable him to prove his innocence. As the years pass that miracle becomes less likely. One is reluctant to write finis to this story, so much so that one almost shares the mental torture which Jeremy Cartland must have suffered. However, one brief footnote to the story may perhaps explain two things: (a) how easy it is for a single unconnected incident to be used as circumstantial evidence against a person and (b) how near one can get to a clue that provides hope, yet still lacks vital evidence.

When the French police seized Jeremy Cartland's belongings they came across a red notebook. In this was an entry which read: 'Play DGR . . . Death of Lizzie. . . . Guilt. . . . Exhumation'. Certainly such an entry in a notebook was curious; after all, Cartland was not a crime reporter, or a policeman, or a pathologist, or even a solicitor. The French police certainly hoped to use these phrases to make allegations against Jeremy, though it is not clear what they were trying to show that he was planning. In fact Cartland was at that time undertaking research into the pre-Raphaelite Brotherhood and the initials DGR stood for Dante Gabriel Rossetti and Lizzie was his wife who committed suicide. The phrase 'Guilt' referred to Rossetti's feelings about his wife's death. As to the word 'exhumation', Rossetti had put several of his poems in his wife's coffin before she was buried. Some years later the coffin was disinterred and the poems recovered and published in 1870.

Cartland stated that a French couple called on his lawyers to say that they would be prepared to give evidence for him if ever his case came to trial, but they did not wish to reveal themselves to the general public as their liaison was not generally known. For this reason they had not gone to the police. Their evidence was that on the night of the murder they were in the vicinity of Pelissane and found themselves driving behind the Cartlands' caravan and a large black Citroen. The latter car made no attempt to overtake the caravan though it was travelling slowly. When the caravan drew off the road much later that night the Citroen did the same. They passed the area sometime afterwards and not only noticed the caravan with all its lights off, but the black Citroen stationary behind some bushes in a lay-by close to the site of the caravan.

But the couple did not take the number of the car and so yet another clue was tantalisingly elusive.

6

'Banned' Donald Woods

'In a small office near passport control they handed me three batches of documents . . . banning me under terms of the Internal Security Act. The banning orders confined me to the magisterial district of East London . . . forbade me to be with more than one person at a time . . .'

DONALD WOODS, writing in *Biko*

As editor of the East London newspaper in South Africa, the *Daily Dispatch*, Donald J. Woods had acquired a considerable reputation as an outspoken critic of *apartheid* and a defender of the black people. The total population of East London during the 1970s was no more than 73,000, which in most countries would hardly support a daily newspaper. But the *Dispatch* had survived and prospered since 1872, and was read with keen interest by many people far beyond East London. It was a newspaper which attracted as much attention in Cape Town and Johannesburg, in Pretoria and Durban, as in its own locality. Indeed, some of its articles caused both anger and heart-searching in government quarters.

Donald Woods was a fifth-generation South African who was born in the Transkei in 1933. He had first of all studied law in Cape Town, but later took up journalism as a career. At the age of thirty-one he was appointed editor of the *Dispatch*, which had become one of the chief critics of *apartheid* in the country. His own column of comment was the most widely syndicated in South Africa. This, as much as anything else, had made him many enemies in the Nationalist Government and on one occasion he was angrily confronted by the Prime Minister, B. J. Vorster, who said: 'The stuff you are writing is stirring the blacks to revolution'.

Woods's father was what was known in South Africa as a trader, but could be described as a small shopkeeper, one who sold all manner of goods from blankets, beads and buckets to spades and tobacco in a tribal reserve. It was, says Woods, 'a home highly conservative on the racial issue', but his proximity to the tribesmen who came to his father's store enabled him to pick up the tribal language at an early age. Over the years his education and a great deal of reading, especially of the works of South Africa's earliest and most eloquent liberal, Alan Paton, brought young Woods to realise the damage which a rigid system of *apartheid* was doing to his homeland.

It was partly at least because of this that he entered journalism. He had some preliminary experience as a journalist overseas, working both in Britain and Canada, and later travelling to the Deep South of the United States to compare segregation there with South Africa. It was perhaps natural in view of his crusading ideals that he should join the *Daily Dispatch* when he returned to South Africa in 1960 because this paper belonged to a charitable foundation, the Crewe Trust, which donated two-thirds of its dividends to charities every year.

The Nationalist Government had been in power since 1948, perhaps far too long a period for any political party in a country which was nominally a democracy, yet whose government practised totalitarian methods as far as the black population was concerned. It meant that the edge of opposition was blunted. The United Party was obviously incapable of being the standard-bearer for the blacks any more than it offered an effective alternative white government. The situation was such that the educated blacks saw no other course than to organise political parties themselves. By 1961 both the ANC (African National Congress) and the PAC (Pan African Congress) had considerable support among the black population. Out of a miasma of hopelessness there arose the glimmering of a Black Consciousness.

This situation was fraught with dangers which hitherto had never threatened South Africa. The intransigence of the Nationalist Government, their refusal to heed what Harold Macmillan had referred to as 'the wind of change' in his efforts to educate Afrikaner opinion to realities, had begun to take its toll. This blindness to the rising tide of black power in other parts of Africa made it easier for the Soviet Union to establish links with the slowly developing political parties of the blacks. The tragedy was that for far too long it was the communist bloc alone which offered any encouragement to their aspirations. Nelson Mandela, leader of the ANC, turned to them for aid. He got it in the form of explosives and firearms as well as cash

The Russians had played a cautious, waiting game in Southern Africa. They made no direct attempts to stir up trouble or foment rebellion as they had done in the former British colonies and in the Congo. They knew that any premature moves on their part would be snuffed out swiftly and ruthlessly by the well-organised secret police of the Nationalist Government. Inevitably, when it was realised that there was aid from Russia coming into the country, the South African Government reacted with stern measures. They had grounds for this not only on account of the financial aid given to certain black groups, but because it was belatedly discovered that the Soviet Union had a well-organised espionage network inside their territory. So the Suppression of Communism Act was introduced and the Government used this as an excuse – sometimes on the flimsiest of evidence – for taking action against black leaders. Often this was done on the pretext that they were only concerned with putting down communism when in fact they were chiefly intent on stifling free speech among the blacks.

Nevertheless the Soviet threat was more serious than many liberals believed. In the late sixties a Soviet spy, Yuri Nikolayevich Loginov, was arrested in Johannesburg. He had been posing as a Canadian citizen under the name of Edmund Trinka. Under interrogation he talked freely to his captors. Major-General Hendrik van den Bergh, South Africa's security chief, was able to say: 'We have a fantastic amount of information and materials in our possession'. This statement was later confirmed by other Western sources. The extent of Loginov's missions and intelligence contacts took in not only South Africa, but Austria, Belgium, Germany, Egypt, Turkey, Kenya, Jordan, Libya, Ethiopa, Tanzania, Iran and Cuba. Loginov had undoubtedly intended to stay in South Africa and build up a network there, for it was disclosed that he had been negotiating with two German immigrants in Johannesburg to become a sleeping partner in their interior decorating business as a cover for his activities.

Thus it can be said that the South African Government had reason to fear subversion by international communist agencies in their own territories. This was certainly one factor in the imprisoning of the leaders of the ANC and the PAC. But many of the Afrikaners' actions went far beyond legitimate concern for national security. Mandela was imprisoned on Robben Island for allegedly planning the violent overthrow of the Nationalist Government. Sobukwe, leader of the PAC, was given a shorter sentence, but when this was completed, he was restricted to living in the remote Kimberley area.

When Mandela and Sobukwe were put into political quarantine, a new leader of the South African blacks arose in the late 1960s. His name was Stephen Biko. He eschewed the personal type of leadership beloved of some African party chiefs and laid the stress on the many he spoke for rather than himself and his lieutenants. Despite this quirk, he was a natural and gifted leader whose logic and powers of persuasion resulted in the development of such movements as SASO (South African Students' Organisation) and BPC (Black People's Convention). Donald Woods gradually became one of Biko's greatest admirers and supporters. As he himself puts it: 'Into this vacuum stepped this unusually gifted man, Bantu Stephen Biko, and he filled it to articulate the aims and philosophy of the black struggle as no black leader had quite been able to do before. He assumed the mantle of leadership unpretentiously and unobtrusively.'

Biko in fact made a tremendous impression on both Donald Woods and his wife, Wendy, who had a similar background to that of her husband, having also been born in the Transkei. They both had a white liberal South African outlook in their opposition to *apartheid*, but, says Donald Woods in his book *Biko*,

thanks to Steve Biko I later came to see that the black struggle had to do with more than the apartheid laws; that his Black Consciousness movement was aimed at psychological oppression as well as legislative oppression . . . and that the entire terms of the struggle generally went beyond the limits envisaged and bounded within the white party political processes.

So Donald Woods's campaign for a fair deal for the blacks was stepped up through the columns of the *Dispatch*. At first there were angry murmurs from some of the white population and attempts at blackmail by advertisers withdrawing their patronage of the newspaper. Vorster had gone out of his way to denounce Woods, but no action had been taken against him. He hoped for immunity from arrest, detention or banning, and for twelve years he achieved this despite his support of the black movement. Meanwhile the Nationalist Government increased its strength among the white population, mainly because the United Party was in many respects merely a pale replica of the Afrikaner-dominated Nationalists. Indeed, the pathetically inept United Party fell into third place in the 1977 election with only ten seats, while the PFP (Progressives), under Helen Suzman, came second with seventeen seats. These figures were far below the Nationalists' 135 seats.

The friendship with Stephen Biko was one based on what Donald Woods himself has described as 'total trust'. This was possible between black and white because Biko, unlike so many black leaders, was not an inverted racist. He did not even hate the Nationalists, only their ideas; indeed he was able coolly and objectively to discuss their complexes. But the writing was on the wall for Biko ever since he had played a major role in defending the cause of nine young blacks who were prosecuted in the Supreme Court of South Africa in 1976 for alleged subversion by intent. Prior to this the Security Police had continually threatened him and his movements had been severely restricted. After the trial of the nine, all of whom were convicted and sentenced to imprisonment for minimum spells of five years, Biko returned to his area of restriction. The following year he and his friend, Peter Jones, were stopped at a Security Police roadblock near Grahamstown and promptly arrested.

The reason for the arrest was that Biko had broken the restriction law by being caught outside his scheduled area. On 6 September 1977, Biko was taken to Room 619 of the Samlam Building in Port Elizabeth. There he was handcuffed, put in leg irons, chained to a grille and interrogated. Exactly what happened during the next few hours nobody other than his inter-rogators can say for certain. But there seems no doubt that he was beaten and possibly even tortured. What is clear was that he fell into a coma and on 13 September news came that he had died in custody.

For Donald Woods the news of Biko's death came like a cold douche. Even he had not realised before the lengths to which some of the Nationalist Establishment would go in their obsessive pursuit of *apartheid* and main-taining a racist society. Antediluvian political prejudice was one thing, but the torture and death of a man who had never harmed anyone was in quite a

Donald Woods reads of the Government's move against him in the very newspaper he was prohibited from editing

Robert Sobukwe, banned leader of the Pan African Congress

Nelson Mandela's wife, Winnie, leads his mother through a Police Cordon

Robben Island, where Mandela is imprisoned

different category. Woods's response to this tragedy was to print in his paper a large picture of Biko with the caption 'We Salute a hero of the nation'.

Biko was not the first black African to have died while in detention. During the sixties more than a score had suffered this fate. Some, like N. Ngudle, A. Madiba and J. Hamakwayo, had committed suicide; a few, like S. Saloojie and A. Timol, had died after leaping out of a high window during interrogation. Others had simply died from causes unknown. But the Biko case was by far the most publicised and there were allegations of criminal brutality by the police interrogators. Biko was only thirty years old when he died, but it is perhaps a measure of the notice which the South African authorities took of his influence among the blacks that in the latter part of his life his movements were restricted, he was forbidden to make speeches, or to speak with more than one person at a time.

The inquest on Biko was totally unsatisfactory. The magistrate who conducted it merely gave his findings that the cause of death was brain injury which led to renal failure and other complications and that his head injuries were 'probably sustained on 7 September in a scuffle in the Security Police offices in Port Elizabeth'. Finally, the inquest court ruled that 'on the available evidence the death cannot be attributed to any act or omission amounting to criminal offence on the part of any person'.

Donald Woods took the view that it was outrageous that the South African Government had not seen fit to conduct a full-scale inquiry into all the circumstances surrounding Biko's death. And in its failure so to act the Government had greatly exacerbated world opinion and earned widespread condemnation. The United States of America, which previously had kept somewhat aloof from African politics, began to show a keener interest in black emancipation movements throughout Southern Africa. When James Kruger, the Nationalist Minister of Justice, replied to criticisms of police brutality not by ordering a public inquiry, but by implying that Biko must have starved himself to death, a few influential liberal-minded Americans began to take a special interest in the Biko case. Donald Woods was invited to go to New York to address the African-American Institute.

Meanwhile Woods had issued a challenge to the Minister of Justice. Returning to the allegations of Biko having died through a hunger strike, he said he would be prepared to resign his post as editor and never write another word for publication if pathologists found that Biko had died of malnutrition or a hunger strike. This promise was made on the understanding that Kruger would give an undertaking to resign from his own office if the pathologists showed that there had been brutality and that the prison officers had deceived the Minister of Justice. The challenge was never taken up.

Then Donald Woods made a speech on the campus of the University of Natal in Pietermaritzburg in which he declared:

South Africa today is ruled by fear – the fear of the ruled and the fear of the rulers.
. . . As always, fear breeds hatred and hatred in turn breeds more fear. . . . South
Africa today is heading for civil war, and we who warn of this endanger ourselves by
doing so, because what we intend as a warning . . . is seen as a kind of advocacy of
the very thing we are trying to prevent.

It was on 22 October 1977 that Donald Woods left home for the airport
on his trip to America. As he reached the passport control desk he handed
his passport to the clerk who was about to stamp it when two plain clothes
men stepped forward and spoke to the fair-haired, middle-aged, bespec-
tacled Donald Woods.

'We are Security Police from headquarters in Pretoria,' they told him. 'I
am afraid you will not be leaving the country on that plane. You are required
to come with us to headquarters.'

Woods had been aware of the risks he was running for some time. The
question was what kind of treatment had the police got in store for him. So
he asked: 'Am I being banned or detained.'

'Banned,' he was told.

They took him away by car and would not let him phone his wife until he
was safely inside headquarters. The police were firm, but polite. They
seemed anxious to avoid any public scene.

At headquarters he was given his banning orders and then motored back
to his home in East London. His suitcase had been searched before being
returned to him. The terms of the banning were that he was to be placed
under surveillance in his home and ordered not to write anything for five
years under threat of imprisonment. This particular order applied not
simply to writing for publication, but even the writing of a manuscript
before it had been published, or even if it was not intended for publication.
The police warned him that they now had the right to call on him at any time
of the day or night to ensure that he was not breaking any of the bans,
which, as well as covering writing, also involved a ban on his being with
more than one person in a room other than his wife or children.

The news of the banning came as a severe shock to Wendy Woods and her
fourteen-year-old daughter Jane, who was old enough to appreciate how it
would affect their home life. From that moment on they would be living a
kind of goldfish bowl existence with not merely the threat of police knock-
ing on their door, but of informers watching their house and every move
they made.

The banning was not, of course, to be compared with similar acts in other
totalitarian systems. There was not the confinement and torture which
typified the methods used in some Latin American countries, nor the
banishment to hard labour or, even worse, to psychiatric hospitals for
brainwashing as under the Soviet system. But for any family who for the
whole of their lives had been under what was supposed to be a civilised and
humane *modus vivendi*, to be treated in this manner in their own homeland

came as a devastating blow. It was as though someone living in Surbiton was to be confined to that area only, banned from working for five years and not allowed more than one visitor at a time, with a positive ban on even a party at Christmas.

Donald Woods had written in his newspaper that

whatever the cause of his [Biko's] death – I repeat, whatever the cause – I hold responsible all those who were associated with his detention without trial. . . . and because Minister J. T. Kruger heads the department which exercises such powers, I hold him particularly accountable in this tragedy.

But a Minister who could commit the indiscretion of saying in public that 'Biko's death leaves me cold' was hardly likely to take kindly to such criticism.

It was a Colonel of the East London Security Police who spelt out in detail the terms of the banning:

From now on, Mr Woods, you are forbidden to travel more than five miles from your home. You must not write for your newspaper and, indeed, you must not write anything at all, even if you don't intend to publish it.

Nor must you go into any school or college, or teach anyone. You must not go into your newspaper office. You must not go into a factory.

'What if I wish to write a letter?'

This question seemed to disconcert the police chief. He was not prepared for it. On reflection he said that perhaps Woods ought to consult a solicitor on this point.

But the police chief enlarged on other consequences of the ban. Woods could not speak to another banned person, nor could he telephone him, and, he warned, from now on it would be illegal for anyone to 'quote' Woods, or to cite what he had said in the past.

Naturally, Woods wanted to know for what reasons he had been banned, though he was quite sure that his newspaper attacks on the Minister of Justice were a prime reason.

'The Minister of Justice is satisfied that you engage in activities which endanger or are calculated to endanger the maintenance of public order,' stated the Colonel. He declined to specify what those activities were.

The Afrikaner mind is not noted for a sophisticated sense of humour and some of the points made by the Security Police and the Colonel bordered on the farcical, though they were quite unable to see them in that light. Donald Woods was banned from playing chess at his club, so he raised the point that it was possible to play chess in a separate room where there would just be himself and his opponent. The Colonel confessed that this was a poser. But, he said, Woods could not drink tea or coffee at the chess club, because drinking these beverages was 'a common social purpose' and that was specifically forbidden. Could he drink tea in a separate room at the club. No was the answer; if everyone else was drinking tea anywhere else in the same building, Woods would still be committing an offence if he drank tea on his own. As to whether he could go to church on Sunday, the Colonel admitted that this was not clearly covered by the terms of the Act, and again he advised Woods to consult a solicitor. As a final shot the Colonel reminded him that he would have to sign the police register every Monday before noon.

Donald Woods first fully realised just how rigorously his banning was being carried out when the police car taking him home drew up outside his door. As he left the car he noticed a black man standing on the opposite side of the road. When the police car pulled away it stopped briefly beside the black man who nodded to the police. The man was unquestionably one of a number of surveillance informers who would from now on keep a close watch on him. It was ironical that the authorities should employ as a spy a man of the very race he most wanted to help.

Perhaps it was at that moment, if only subconsciously, that Donald must have realised that his only hope was somehow, sometime to escape from this five-year nightmare. But first he had to keep a brave, smiling face for his family. He was warmly greeted by his wife, Wendy, daughter Jane and their other three children, eleven-year-old Duncan, Gavin, aged nine, and Mary, five. Not the least demonstrative was Charlie, their black Labrador.

The telephone rang and Wendy Woods told her husband how scores of people had been ringing up to inquire what had happened. That brought another realisation: the telephone, the prime tool after a typewriter of the journalist's craft, was now certain to be tapped and, to be on the safe side, Wendy would have to answer it and do most of the talking. And, of course, if the doorbell rang, or anyone knocked, Donald must not answer it. There might be more than one person outside and if the surveillance man reported that, he could be held to have broken the ban.

The more he contemplated the real results of the ban, the more he realised what daily irritations were to be piled upon him. Worse than that, it would be a constant source of frustration for the whole family. No longer could they keep open house and that involved all manner of restrictions for the children, too. It was the effect it would have on the children which greatly worried Donald.

For any man to be robbed of his work, especially of work he loves, is bad enough, but for Donald there was also the knowledge that his crusade on behalf of oppressed blacks was silenced. As far as they were concerned he was now totally useless.

The real strain was mainly on his wife who, though a dedicated supporter of all Donald stood for, had the responsibility of making many of the decisions which normally he would have taken himself. If any friends

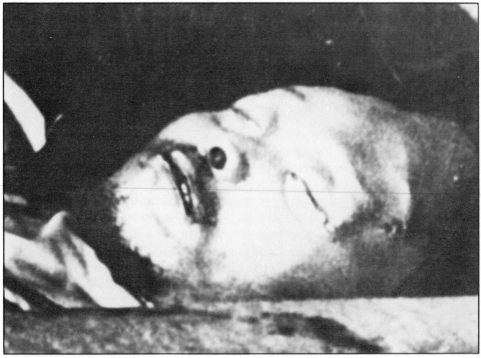

The dead face of Steve Biko who died while in Police custody in Pretoria

King Williamstown: a rally held before Steve Biko's burial

James Kruger, the Minister for Justice

Ntsiki Biko with her 2 children. 'Steve may be dead but his struggle will continue'

wanted to call on them, Wendy had the job of saying yes or no and making suitable excuses when the answer had to be in the negative. Sometimes there would be inquiries from an American newspaperman wanting to have information and once an American TV company sent a reporter and cameraman to interview her rather than her husband. In such circumstances any little slip-up, or forgetfulness of the implications of the ban, could have wrought havoc on the Woods household.

Fortunately the *Daily Dispatch* continued to pay Donald Woods his salary and supported him in every possible way. But as each day passed and as anger gave way to a philosophical approach to his predicament, Woods was able to realise how very much he was a prisoner. Had he been an ordinary black man undergoing the ordeal of a banning order, it would have been much worse. Then he would almost certainly have been denied even a livelihood. Banning was a subtle weapon, a destroyer of one's morale, something which in the end could easily make one just as much a defeatist as the liberal white citizen who decided there was nothing he could do to change the present political situation in South Africa.

At first he spent much of the day sitting at his piano in shorts and playing Chopin sonatas. In between times he would watch television, or read, but all the time he missed not being able to write. Wendy Woods not only had to answer the telephone, but to contend with dozens of threatening telephone calls, all intended to demoralise the family. In one day alone there were five bomb threats. Slogans were painted on the walls of their house, phrases such as 'Biko Commy HQ'; there were equally threatening letters, sometimes composed in the filthiest phraseology. Once shots were fired at the house. Each time Donald went outside the house into their garden he saw the black man who was a police spy in his usual place across the road, pretending to read a newspaper.

Occasionally, when visitors came to the house, Woods would try to make a joke of it all. Some of their friends did not altogether appreciate the situation and felt convinced that Donald would not have been banned unless he had been a Communist. Wendy repeatedly had to try to convince them that he was not a Communist and that this was not why he was banned. She had to point out that if any of them wanted a quick word with him, they would have to go into his room one at a time. Donald would joke through the half-open door that he had better not come in, as 'I might contaminate you all'. Sometimes he put a leg through the half open door and said, 'Look, now I'm breaking the ban'.

But a sense of humour was insufficient for him to sustain this kind of life for long. Apart from playing the piano, chess and watching television, all he could do, he used to say, was to 'get in Wendy's way'.

His lawyer had a lengthy discussion with the magistrate concerning the banning order, as to what Woods could or could not do. At first the magistrate insisted that he could not go to church at all. Why did he want to go to church every Sunday? Because he was a Roman Catholic and they were supposed to do this. Very grudgingly it was later conceded that he could go to church. There was the strange anomaly that he could not go to rugby matches because he wouldn't be on his own, but he could attend cricket matches provided he sat away from the crowd.

'You had better not push for too many concessions,' his lawyer told him, 'because they may counteract this by slapping on more restrictions. The other day in the Transvaal there was a case where a banned person was forbidden to be in the same room even with one other person.'

The Woods family eventually began to feel sorry for the black police informer who patiently waited across the road each day. No doubt he hated being a police spy, but what could he do? He needed work and if he refused this, all manner of proceedings could be taken against him. Once, from the gates of their home, Wendy looked across at the man and he gave a half-smile and shrugged his shoulders as much as to say, 'I'm just carrying out orders'.

Even Wendy's movements were watched by the police when she left the house. A police car would wait while she was shopping or when she went to a friend's house and sometimes follow her home. When she went to the bank to cash a cheque, the clerk would leave the counter to make inquiries before he gave her the money. It was clear that the bank had had instructions from the Security Police to consult them before cashing a cheque of more than a certain figure. They knew the telephone was tapped and their mail intercepted, but what they could not be sure about was whether any listening devices had been installed in the house or grounds.

It was about ten days after the banning order that Donald took one important decision. He was determined to carry on with his writing in secret; that at least would be an antidote to his boredom and sense of frustration. He could feel that he was still doing something worthwhile. So, despite the order banning him from writing, he decided on 1 November 1977 to write a book about Stephen Biko and all he had stood for. 'The manuscript had, therefore, to be written in secret, subject to frequent interruptions and alarms, since every knock at the door and every approaching footfall could mean the arrival of Security Police,' he wrote in *Biko*. He found this task both exhilarating and unnerving, but he wanted to set things down while his memories of Biko were fresh and concise, before the details became blurred in his mind. Somehow he hoped he would be able to smuggle the manuscript to London and perhaps it could be published.

When he discussed this possibility with Wendy, they both agreed that this posed a new question altogether, one they had avoided talking about before, but which had been uppermost in their minds – the stark truth that eventually they would need to leave the country. And as long as the ban remained this meant the only way they could do it would be by escaping. It would, of course, mean seeking an entirely new life elsewhere, starting afresh in London or New York, or possibly some provincial city in either Britain or the USA.

For a while the idea of escape remained just a dream, something which they might contemplate later on. But one day the whole family was shattered by an incident which forced both Donald and Wendy to decide that the dream must be put into practice.

A parcel arrived addressed to the youngest Woods child, five-year-old Mary. She opened it and found a T-shirt with a print of Steve Biko on the front. She decided to put it on and suddenly the sound of her screams brought everyone into the room. Mary was struggling with the T-shirt half over her face, crying out 'My eyes! My eyes!' Her sister pulled the shirt over her head and saw that Mary's hands and face were purple. As Donald Woods picked up the shirt to examine it, white powder fell on to the floor. The T-shirt had been sent to Mary by a genuine sympathiser of the family. But it must have been intercepted somewhere *en route* and sprinkled with ninhydrin, an acid-based substance used by police to lift fingerprints from paper. There was no doubt that this had been done by someone in the Security Police after they had intercepted the mail at the sorting office.

This totally unexpected and vicious attack made Donald realise that from now on it was not just he and Wendy who were under attack, but their children, too. That made up his mind that somehow they must plan an escape for the whole family. They could not subject the children to living under such conditions. And if Donald's book about Biko was published, they would have to go in any case.

They dared not tell any of their friends about their plan to escape. Nor dared they tell the children in case one of them unwittingly let something drop in casual conversation with their friends. For that matter, as Woods wisely pointed out, they could not safely discuss it among themselves in the house, in case they were bugged. So some of these preliminary talks on escape were conducted in the garden.

An attempt was made to find the perpetrators of the outrage on Mary and evidence was actually collected after some difficulty. This was handed over to the Security Police with a formal complaint, but nothing was done about it. This only strengthened their resolve to get away. So plans were made in great secrecy and by the Wednesday morning of 28 December Donald and Wendy were in a position to fix the following evening as their deadline for beginning the great escape. It was agreed that this had to be done in two separate stages, first with Donald on his own, and afterwards, but before his escape could be discovered, the rest of the family.

The planning had to be meticulous because there was a very real risk that if Donald Woods was caught before he left the country, his family would be in danger of arrest. Similarly, they dared not make any premature move which might arouse the suspicions of the police and put them on Donald's trail. There was one slight complication: Jane, their eldest daughter, had been invited to spend the weekend with friends. It was obviously impossible for her to do this, or all the escape plans would be jeopardised. Donald, who was able to drive his car within the five-mile limit, took Jane for a spin on some simple pretext, then stopped the car and told her to get out.

'Listen carefully,' he told his perplexed daughter, 'you must not go to your friends this weekend.'

'But why, Daddy? And why have we got out of the car?'

'We have got out of the car because it is just possible it might have a bug planted in it somewhere and all we say would be recorded by the Security Police. But the truth is that we are in danger if we live in South Africa any longer. So we are going to escape – to England or America. But you mustn't breathe a word of this to anyone.'

It was shock for Jane. She loved South Africa, its countryside, her friends and her family's way of life in that country. To have to contemplate leaving it, perhaps for ever, was sickening.

Donald had two friends who were absolutely trustworthy and in whom he had confided his intention to escape. He had made this one concession in not telling their plans to anyone because he realised that some outside aid was needed. To escape entirely on his own would be foolhardy. One of these men had thought of flying all the Woods family out of South Africa in a light aircraft, but had to abandon this plan for a variety of reasons. But the other friend suggested that by far the simplest plan was to escape on foot. Having studied the maps for the best possible route, it dawned on them that East London was only a little more than two hundred miles from the borders of Lesotho, the land-locked independent kingdom surrounded on all sides by South African territory. This territory had once been Basutoland, which had received British protection in 1869 at the request of Moshesh, the first paramount chief. In 1871 the land had been annexed to the Cape Colony, but in 1884 it was restored to the direct control of the British Government. Finally, in 1966, Basutoland became an independent and sovereign member of the Commonwealth under the title of the Kingdom of Lesotho. Thus it was outside South Africa's jurisdiction and, once there, Donald Woods could fly to London.

One friend whom, for the purposes of this narrative and in the cause of security, we shall call Drew agreed to drive Woods to the border. The other said he would assist in any way possible. After carefully studying the maps and realising that once he was in Lesotho he would be among friends, Woods fell in with the plan.

There was one snag – getting across the Lesotho border without going through customs. They discussed using two cars, one driven by Donald and one going ahead, with a two-way walkie-talkie radio set which would enable the first car to warn the second if there were any road blocks. Woods realised that in the area between East London and the Lesotho border the police erected road blocks from time to time to inspect cars for the smuggling of marijuana. If they could reach the Lesotho border at night time, it might be feasible to avoid the border post by walking over the Lesotho hills and down to the main Maseru road.

Yet the gamble was still a considerable one. It would for example be too dangerous to drive to the Woods's home and somehow to smuggle Donald into the car. The informer, or the Security Police themselves, would almost certainly make a note of the number of the car and its driver. So it was arranged that Donald must disguise himself as professionally as he could on his own, dying his hair and putting on unfamiliar clothes, get into their car, lie down on the floor out of sight, and his wife would drive him away to a safe point outside the town where he could be left. Then he could walk or hitch-hike to a point where he could be picked up and taken to the border.

Wendy would then return straight home and let it be known as widely as possible that very early the following morning she would be driving with her children to her parents' home in Umtata, about a hundred and fifty miles distant. There they would await a telephone call from Donald saying he was safely inside Lesotho. Once they had that news it would be perfectly safe for them to drive straight to the border of Lesotho as ordinary tourists and cross over. Lesotho was only about a hundred miles from Umtata, not as long a journey as from East London, and the Security Police would be highly unlikely to have discovered Donald's disappearance by that time.

There were, of course, a lot of 'if's' and 'but's'. In theory the plan could work quite smoothly. But supposing Donald Woods had not telephoned by ten a.m.? Supposing again that for some reason the police became suspicious, made inquiries, called at the house and found he had gone? It was agreed that they must take the risk that a Security Police officer might unexpectedly call at the house. But the whole escape plan hinged on Woods being able to telephone his wife by ten a.m. If that call did not come through, then the family must assume that the plan had failed, or he had been caught. They must then return to East London at once, pretending they knew nothing of what had happened.

But by 28 December they felt that all possible precautions had been taken and all risks carefully weighed up. That the escape plan had been put into operation very cautiously may be judged from the fact that originally they had hoped to make the getaway on Christmas Eve, believing that this was one occasion when customs guards and police would be least wary and perhaps in a mellower frame of mind. But because some tiny details had not been thrashed out they had waited until after the Christmas holiday before positively fixing the date. In the previous few days they had deliberately telephoned various friends making plans to see them in the coming year and making imaginary dates in the months ahead. If the police were listening in, then they hoped this would lead them to believe that they had no plans to escape.

By this time, too, the Biko book was finished and Woods packed a copy of the typescript into his case along with a change of clothes and a revolver. He had already smuggled one copy of the typescript in small batches at a time to a friend in London but he could not be sure whether all had arrived safely. Packing the revolver was not a question of shooting one's way out of the country, but a necessary precaution against bandits on the lonely Lesotho roads.

Waiting for the actual moment of making the first move was the worst ordeal of all. During the hours before the getaway Donald went over and over the various options offered by the escape plan and the many things that could go wrong. He realised that if he was caught, or indeed if they were all caught, it would be years before Wendy and he would see one another again. Then there was the problem of money. They could not get any of their funds transferred from South Africa, so they just had to leave the bulk of their savings behind, taking with them a very small pittance so that no suspicions were aroused by large withdrawals from the bank.

It hurt Donald to have to keep his plans secret from so many of his friends, but he felt strongly that the less they knew the safer they would be from police investigations. Secrecy was as much in their best interests as his own. It was equally essential that those who were helping him were shielded from the police. Perhaps his greatest regret was that he dared not let Helen, their faithful black servant, know what was going on. Wendy rang her closest woman friend and mentioned during the conversation that Donald was going to bed early that night and she was taking her children to the beach.

Donald had hit upon the idea of disguising himself as a priest so that if necessary he could cross into Lesotho from a Catholic mission station near the border. He had dyed his hair and put on a dark suit, clerical collar and black cravat and, while Helen was sent off into the garden on an errand for Wendy, he slipped quietly into the garage. There he clambered into the car and crouched down on the floor out of sight.

Wendy opened the garage doors and reversed the car out, heading away from East London into the country. All the time she kept a wary eye on the driving mirror to make sure she was not being followed. Occasionally she had known her car to be followed discreetly by the Security Police and she dared not take any risks on this occasion.

A short distance along a country road Donald and Wendy said goodbye and he then hitch-hiked to the point where Drew was waiting for him with the two cars, each with a walkie-talkie radio.

Drew drove the first car and Donald followed in the second. They kept in touch by radio, though on one occasion they momentarily lost contact. Suddenly Woods noticed the lights of a van which was travelling behind them. He was convinced it was a police van and informed Drew of this over the radio. Drew's advice was that he should slow down and let the van pass. This he did, but the van slowed down, too. Drew, who kept remarkably cool, told him to slow down more. At last the van shot past them and all sighed with relief.

Then the front wheel of the Woods's car was punctured, and Donald radioed Drew to tell him what had happened. Drew drove back to help change the wheel. Once or twice a car came along and, to be on the safe side, Woods dived into the ditch to keep out of range of its headlights. At last they had the wheel fixed and were ready to go, but Woods had suffered two drenchings in the ditch and was beginning to feel uncomfortably wet.

Once again they set off, this time approaching the Lesotho border and the Telle River. As they got closer to the border so the road became progressively worse, and in places was little better than a rough mud track full of holes. They had been driving for eight hours and, mainly because of the puncture, were an hour behind schedule. The original plan had been for Donald to wade across the Telle River and then hike over the hills to meet a friend waiting for him in Lesotho on the Maseru Road. But one look at the state of the river showed that plans would have to be revised. Not only had valuable time been lost, but the river, which at this time should have been shallow enough for a crossing on foot, was now swollen and deep after several days of incessant rain.

Nor did there seem to be any possibility of a boat. They now wished they had somehow secured a rubber dinghy. Donald felt that the best plan was for him alone to try to find some way over the border and for Drew to go back. They shook hands, Drew saying that if Woods needed help he could knock on the door of one of the huts of the blacks nearby. He also said that the second car wouldn't be a problem – he would have help collecting it.

There was indeed not much else Donald Woods could do but hope and pray. The border and safety lay so close ahead and yet he was very far from being safe himself. He was still worried that by some mishap at home his absence might have been discovered and that there was a police car out looking for him. Drew drove off and Woods picked up his bag and headed for the huts.

It took some time for a sleepy and suspicious black African to recognise Woods in his current disguise but once he knew who it was he gladly asked him into the hut, made some coffee and offered to show him the best and safest crossing-point. The African, Tami, had an old crock of a car that was almost falling apart, but he managed to drive Donald down to the river again. This new crossing-point was certainly much safer than the previous one and there was a fair chance of wading across. Woods had to weigh the risks of possible failure in making the crossing with the fact that he had lost so much time that, if he succeeded in making his rendezvous with his friend, they could not possibly get to Maseru by ten o'clock. The alternative was to risk going through the border post – he had a forged passport for such a contingency. So he shook hands with Tami and waded across to the patrol point. The gates were locked and no one was in sight.

Donald rattled the gates and banged on them with his fist. All was silent. He banged again and this time called out. Eventually a black policeman came out of the hut to see who it was. Donald inquired why the gate was locked, and was informed that it was not opened until seven o'clock in the morning.

Woods, who was still in the guise of a Roman Catholic clergyman, hoped for some consideration by pleading that he had to say early mass in Qthing just over the border.

'I'm very sorry, reverend,' replied the black policeman, 'but there is nothing I can do. Even if I was allowed to let you in, there is nobody to stamp your papers until seven o'clock.' With that he returned to the hut.

Impatiently, Donald strode up and down outside the gates, worried about making the deadline of ten o'clock when he had to telephone his family and all this wasted time. Then he saw a car approaching the gates and, as the outline was that of a Land Rover, he feared it might be the police. It was with real relief that he saw it was being driven by a black man. They exchanged greetings as the newcomer pulled up by the gates.

'Where are you going?' inquired the black.

'To say mass in Qthing,' replied Woods.

'Jump in the car and sit here while you are waiting. We'll cross over together and I'll give you a lift.'

It seemed an age before the gates were opened and even then it was a few minutes after seven o'clock. They drove through the gates and halted inside by the hut. Two officials inspected the black's papers and Woods's forged passport. Donald was given a form to fill in and then the passport was stamped and he was waved out of the hut. For a moment he felt so elated that he started to do a little jig with sheer delight. But he noticed the policeman looking at him in some astonishment and quickly stopped. He supposed it must seem very strange for a sober clergyman to be doing a jig.

At last he was into Lesotho. All that now remained was to make that telephone call as soon as possible.

All this time Wendy Woods had been anxiously passing the hours waiting for Donald's call and hoping all would go smoothly. She had destroyed a whole mass of papers at home, burning anything that might incriminate either them or their friends after they had got away. She had done all the packing and coped with inquisitive questions from the younger children from whom the whole plan had been kept secret. There were so very many questions she could not answer, such as why she was packing warm clothes, and why wasn't Daddy up and about.

At last they all got into the car and drove away. Perhaps the saddest moment for Wendy Woods was when Charlie, their dog, chased the car out of the drive. They could not take it with them. The black police informer for once was sitting down and nodding off to sleep.

But there was trouble with the car and the journey took far longer than

183

Donald Woods, his wife Wendy and their five children safe in Britain after their dramatic escape from South Africa (from l. to r.) Jane (14), Duncan (11), Dillon (13), Mary (6) and Gavin (9)

Wendy ever expected. While Donald was fretting as to whether he would make it to a telephone box by ten o'clock, his wife was worrying herself sick in case she did not arrive by the time the call came through. Eventually she arrived at her parents' home with only twenty minutes to spare.

Donald was given a lift along the road to Maseru and managed to link up with his friend. It was only by a lucky chance that they made their rendez-vous as neither man had realised there were so many roads into Maseru. By great good fortune each had chosen the same route. As they ruefully admitted afterwards maps were not much help in this part of the world. Woods got to the British High Commissioner's office in Maseru ten minutes before the deadline. Within a few minutes he had put through a phone call to Wendy to let her know he had arrived safely. Mrs Woods and the children then set out immediately for Lesotho and by dusk that day the whole family was reunited and the South African Security Police had still not learned of their escape.

Woods explained to the High Commissioner that he and his family were escaping from South Africa and planned to go to Britain. From Lesotho he was able to arrange for a charter aircraft to fly them to Gaberone in Botswana and then on to Zambia, finally getting a plane from Lusaka to London. The great adventure of escape was over at last, but the new adventure of starting a new life in a strange country was about to begin. It was not an easy adventure because the Woods had had to leave behind their savings and many of their belongings.

Through all their hardships and the problems they encountered in sett-ling down in their new surroundings, Donald Woods has never regretted the decision he took. In his bag he brought with him a typescript of his work on Biko. In London he was able to revise and edit the book and it was eventually published – not just as a biography or picture of Biko as a man and black African leader, but, as he put it, as part of a crusade 'to help finish the work of Steve Biko . . . so that chains may be broken wherever they hold in bondage the bodies and minds of men'.

Today he has the gratification of seeing this crusade upheld and sus-tained. The name of Stephen Biko and his Black Consciousness movement has been blazoned across three continents. But Donald Woods's campaign has won many adherents not only in Britain and America, but also inside South Africa itself, and indeed even among Afrikaners. André Brink, an Afrikaner novelist, has laid himself open to a campaign of such vilification and physical threat as a 'traitorous Afrikaner' that he and his family have had to be especially vigilant in all moves they make outside their home. Fortunately for Brink, he lives in the relative quiet of Grahamstown where the Security Police are not as brutal as in other parts of the Union. Since Donald Woods left his native country, the South African Government has tightened up on some of its laws. The Police Act, passed in 1979, provides that any citizen can be prosecuted for publishing anything reflecting badly on police behaviour without first obtaining permission from the police authorities. Thus Brink can be convicted for writing even a work of fiction which reflects on the Security Police.

But, writing of Brinks, Donald Woods says there is an Afrikaans proverb to comfort heroes under attack: 'It is the tallest trees which catch the most wind'.

Bibliography

Brink, André, *A Dry White Season* (W. H. Allen, London, 1979).
Cartland, Jeremy, *The Cartland File* (Linkline Publications, Brighton, 1978).
Cookridge, E. H., *The Third Man* (Arthur Barker, London, 1968).
Hamilton, Peter, *Espionage, Terrorism, & Subversion in an Industrial Society* (Peter A. Heims, Leatherhead, 1979).
Hinds, Alfred, *In Contempt of Court* (Bodley Head, London, 1966).
John, Otto, *I Came Home Twice, Twice through the Lines* translated by R. H. Berry (Macmillan, London, 1972).
Koch, Peter & Hermann, Kai, *Assault at Mogadishu*, translated and edited by John Man (Corgi Books, London, 1977).
Lucas, Norman, *The Lucan Mystery* (W. H. Allen, London, 1975).
Maclean, Fitzroy, *Take Nine Spies* (Weidenfeld & Nicolson, London, 1978).
McCormick, Donald, *The Master Book of Escapes* (Hodder Causton, London, 1974).
Page, Bruce; Leitch, David & Knightley, Phillip, *Philby: The Spy Who Betrayed a Generation* (André Deutsch, London 1968).
Philby, Eleanor, *Kim Philby: The Spy I Loved* (Hamish Hamilton, London, 1969).
Philby, Kim (H. A. R.), *My Silent War* (MacGibbon & Kee, London, 1968).
Trevor-Roper, Hugh, *The Philby Affair* (William Kimber, London, 1968).
Wise, David & Ross, Thomas B., *The Espionage Establishment* (Random House, New York, 1967).
Woods, Donald, *Biko* (Paddington Press, London, 1978).

ALSO CONSULTED

Reports of the Small Situation Management Group on the Mogadishu hijacking; official reports of the West German Federal Criminal Police; report of a conversation between an official from the Federal Chancellor's Office with Andreas Baader; Files of *The Times, Daily Express, Daily Mail, News of the World, Der Spiegel, Stern Magazin*.

Acknowledgements

The publishers would like to thank the following for their help and co-operation in preparing this book: Alfred Hinds, Donald Woods and Jeremy Cartland.

They acknowledge their use of copyright material from the following publications: *My Silent War* by Kim Philby, Granada Publishing Ltd; *The Philby Affair* by Hugh Trevor-Roper, William Kimber & Co Ltd reprinted by permission of A. D. Peters & Co Ltd; *Take Nine Spies* by Sir Fitzroy Maclean, Weidenfeld & Nicolson Ltd; *In Contempt of Court* by Alfred Hinds, The Bodley Head; *Biko* by Donald Woods, Paddington Press Ltd; *The Cartland File* by Jeremy Cartland, Linkline Publications.

Picture research by Diana Souhami. The picture credits are as follows: Associated Press 14, 15 (top left), 20 (bottom right), 34, 116, 169 (top right and bottom), 174 (bottom left); Camera Press 15 (top right), 35, 184; Jeremy Cartland 142, 143 (top), 148 (bottom), 149 (bottom), 154 (top), 155 (bottom); Keystone 15 (bottom), 20 (bottom left), 91 (bottom), 96 (bottom), 105 (top right), 168, 174 (top), 175; Mirrorpic 44 (bottom), 54, 55 (bottom), 63 (top), 67; Pix Features 104, 105 (top left and bottom), 117, 122, 123, 128, 129, 132, 133, 174 (bottom right); Popperfoto 20 (top), 62, 63 (bottom), 96 (top left), 113, 149 (top); Press Association 112; Syndication International 21, 44 (top), 45, 55 (top), 66, 97 (top right), 143 (bottom), 148 (top), 154 (bottom), 155 (top).

Index

INDEX